First World War

and Army of Occupation

War Diary

France, Belgium and Germany

42 DIVISION
Divisional Troops
Divisional Trench Mortar Batteries
1 April 1917 - 31 January 1919

WO95/2649/4

The Naval & Military Press Ltd
www.nmarchive.com
Published in association with The National Archives

Published by

The Naval & Military Press Ltd

Unit 10 Ridgewood Industrial Park,
Uckfield, East Sussex,
TN22 5QE England
Tel: +44 (0) 1825 749494

www.naval-military-press.com
www.nmarchive.com

This diary has been reprinted in facsimile from the original. Any imperfections are inevitably reproduced and the quality may fall short of modern type and cartographic standards.

Contents

War Diary	Bus. O24. A8.3. France Sheet 57C	25/08/1917	25/08/1917
War Diary	Bau Paunne	26/08/1917	26/08/1917
War Diary	Proven	27/08/1917	27/08/1917
War Diary	Watou K9.C 8.5	29/08/1917	29/08/1917
War Diary	Vlamertinghe H7.C.3.4 Sheet 28	30/08/1917	31/08/1917
War Diary	Havrincourt Wood P18.b.1.8 France Sheet 57C.	04/08/1917	20/08/1917
War Diary	Bus O.24. A 8.3.	25/08/1917	25/08/1917
War Diary	Baupaunne	26/08/1917	26/08/1917
War Diary	Proven	27/08/1917	27/08/1917
War Diary	Watou K9.C.8.5. Sheet 27.	29/08/1917	29/08/1917
War Diary	Vlamertinghe Sheet 28	30/08/1917	30/09/1917
War Diary	Vlamertinghe H 8.C.7.6. Sheet 28	01/09/1917	30/09/1917
Heading	War Diary Of 42nd Divn Trench Mortars. R.A. From 1st October 1917 To 31st October 1917 Volume VII		
War Diary	Wormhoudt	01/10/1917	01/10/1917
War Diary	Teteghem	02/10/1917	02/10/1917
War Diary	Coxyde Bains W6. C 8.8.	03/10/1917	13/10/1917
War Diary	Coxyde X13. B.7.8 Sheet 11 S.E.	13/10/1917	16/10/1917
War Diary	Headquarters. Coxyde X13. B.7.8. Sheet II.S.E.	17/10/1917	25/10/1917
War Diary	Coxyde X13. B.7.8. Sheet II.S.E.	30/10/1917	31/10/1917
War Diary	Coxyde Headquarters X 13. B.7.8 Sheet II S.E.	26/10/1917	31/10/1917
Heading	War Diary Of 42nd Divisional. Trench Mortar Brigade R.A. From November 1st 1917 To November 30th 1917 Volumn VIII		
War Diary	Coxyde X13. B.7.8.	01/11/1917	01/11/1917
War Diary	Belgium Sheet II. S.E. 1:20,000	01/11/1917	03/11/1917
War Diary	Coxyde X13 C.7.8 Sheet II S.E. 1/20,000	04/11/1917	16/11/1917
War Diary	Coxyde X 13b.78	17/11/1917	22/11/1917
War Diary	Fontes	30/11/1917	30/11/1917
War Diary	Calonne Sur-La-Lys. Franch Sheet 36A	30/11/1917	30/11/1917
Heading	War Diary Of 42nd Trench Mortar Brigade R.A. From 1st December 1917 To 31st December 1917 Vol IX.		
Miscellaneous	The Staff Captain R.A. R.A. Headquarters 42/Div.	31/12/1917	31/12/1917
War Diary	Beuvry. P20.a.8.9	03/12/1917	03/12/1917
War Diary	Bethune Combined Sheet 36A SE 36 S.W. 36A N.E. 36B N.W. France 1:40,000	04/12/1917	06/12/1917
War Diary	Beuvry F20.a. 8.9.	07/12/1917	13/12/1917
War Diary	Beuvry Headquarters. F20.a.8.9.	13/12/1917	13/12/1917
War Diary	Bethune Combined Sheet 36A S.E. 36 S.W. 36c NE 36c N.W.	14/12/1917	16/12/1917
War Diary	Beuvry F20.a.8.9.	17/12/1917	21/12/1917
War Diary	Beuvry F20.a.8.9 Bethune Combined Sheet France 1:40,000	21/12/1917	31/12/1917
Heading	War Diary Of 42nd Division Trench Mortar Brigade R.A. From 1st January 1918. To 31st January 1918. Volume X		
War Diary	Le Preol Headquarters F10 C.5.2 Bethune Combined Sheet (36 A.S.E. 36 S.W. 36 Bne 36c N.W. 1:40,000	01/01/1918	02/01/1918
War Diary	Le Preol	02/01/1918	30/01/1918
Heading	War Diary Of 42nd Div. Trench Mortars. R.A. From 1.2.1918 To 28.2.1918. Vol XI		
War Diary	Le Preol Headquarters F10b 5.2. Bethune Combined Sheet 36A S.E. 36 S.W. 36c NE 36c N.W. 1:4000	03/12/1917	03/12/1917
War Diary	Le Preol	04/02/1918	16/02/1918
War Diary	Vendin Les Bethune E4a.4.4. Bethune Combined Sheet 1:40,000	17/02/1918	27/02/1918

Heading	D.T.M.O. 42nd Divisional Trench Mortars. March 1918		
Heading	War Diary Of 42nd Div Trench Mortars R.A. From 1st March 1918 To 31st March 1918 Vol XIII		
War Diary	Vendin Les Bethune E4.A. Bethune Combined Sheet 1:40,000	01/03/1918	17/03/1918
War Diary	Gonnehem V18C.8.4.	18/03/1918	24/03/1918
War Diary	Monehy au Bois	25/03/1918	25/03/1918
War Diary	Gaudiempre	27/03/1918	31/03/1918
Heading	42nd Division Trench Mortars. R.A. April 1918		
Heading	War Diary of 42nd Division Trenches Mortars R.A. From 1.4.18 To 30.4.18. Volume XIII		
War Diary	Gaudiempre	01/04/1918	02/04/1918
War Diary	Souastre D 15 d.9.1.	03/04/1918	05/04/1918
War Diary	Hannescamps E10 b 2.8. Sheet 57D N.E.	06/04/1918	17/04/1918
War Diary	Headquarters Couin J 1 D 55.35	17/04/1918	17/04/1918
War Diary	Couin J1 D 55.35.	17/04/1918	30/04/1918
Heading	War Diary Of 42nd Division Trench Mortars. R.A. From May 1st 1918. To May 31st 1918. Volume XIV		
War Diary	Headquarters Couin J 1 D 55.35 Sheet 57 D N.E.	01/05/1918	31/05/1918
Heading	War Diary Of 42nd. Div. Trench Mortars R.A. From 1.6.1918 To 30.6.1918. Volume XV		
War Diary	Headquarters. Couin J1d 55.35. Sheet 57 D N.E.	01/06/1918	17/06/1918
War Diary	Couin J 1d 55.35.	17/06/1918	29/06/1918
War Diary	Bus. J26d 55.65 Sheet 57 D.N.E. 1:20,000	30/06/1918	30/06/1918
War Diary	Bus-Les-Artois J 26 d 55.65 Sheet 57 D. N.E	30/06/1918	30/06/1918
Heading	War Diary Of 42nd Divisional Trench Mortars R.A. From 1st July 1918 to 31st July 1918 Volume XVI		
War Diary	Bus-Les-Artois J26d55.85 1:20,000 Sheet 57 D. N.E	01/07/1918	06/07/1918
War Diary	Bus-Les Artois.	07/07/1918	31/07/1918
Heading	War Diary Of 42nd. Division Trench Mortars R.A. From 1st August 1918 To 31st August 1915. Volume XVIII		
War Diary	Bus Les Artois J 26d 55.85 1:20,000 Sheet 27 D. N.E.	01/08/1918	07/08/1918
War Diary	Bus Les Artois	08/08/1918	28/08/1918
War Diary	Miraumont	30/08/1918	30/08/1918
Heading	War Diary Of 42nd. Trench Mortars. R.A. From 1.9.1918. To 30.9.18. Volume XVIII.		
War Diary	Miraumont	01/09/1918	01/09/1918
War Diary	Grevillers	02/09/1918	03/09/1918
War Diary	Riencourt	04/09/1918	04/09/1918
War Diary	Barastre O15.a 70.25. Sheet. 57.C.	04/09/1918	21/09/1918
War Diary	Ruyaulcourt P 10 d.05. 50. Sheet 57C.	22/09/1918	30/09/1918
Heading	War Diary Of 42nd. Divisional Trench Mortars R.A. From 1st October 1918. 31st October 1918 Volume XIX		
War Diary	Royaulcourt P 10 d 05.50 Sheet 57.c.	02/10/1918	02/10/1918
War Diary	Trescault Q 4a 76.50	03/10/1918	10/10/1918
War Diary	Lesdain N2 b.0.8. Sheet 57.B.	11/10/1918	12/10/1918
War Diary	Beauvois En Cambresis. I 9.d.3.3.	12/10/1918	13/10/1918
War Diary	Beauvois	15/10/1918	15/10/1918
War Diary	Beauvois I 11c.50.05. Sheet 57c	16/10/1918	16/10/1918
War Diary	Quievy D 19c 85.25. Sheet 57B.	17/10/1918	22/10/1918
War Diary	Briastre D 24c 85.30. Sheet 57B.	22/10/1918	23/10/1918
War Diary	Solesmes D 12 b 50.80	25/10/1918	27/10/1918
War Diary	Romeries W21c 95.15 Sheet 51A S.E	27/10/1918	31/10/1918

Heading	War Diary Of 42nd. Div. Trench Mortars. R.A. From 1.11.1918 To 30.11.18. Volume XX.		
War Diary	Romeries W21c95.15 Sheet 51A. S.E.	01/11/1918	06/11/1918
War Diary	Villereau M28c 40.80 Sheet 51	07/11/1918	12/11/1918
War Diary	Pont. Sur. Sambre O33.c.7.2.	30/11/1918	30/11/1918
War Diary	Romeries W 21b 95.15 Sheet 51 A. S.E.	01/11/1918	06/11/1918
War Diary	Villereau M28b 40.80 Sheet 51	07/11/1918	12/11/1918
War Diary	Pont-Sur-Sambre O33.c.7.2	13/11/1918	30/11/1918
Heading	War Diary Of 42nd. Div Trench Mortars. R.A. From 1.12.1918 To 31st 12.1918 Volume XXI		
War Diary	La Haute Rue	01/12/1918	13/12/1918
War Diary	Pont-Sur-Sambre	14/12/1918	14/12/1918
War Diary	Marpent	15/12/1918	15/12/1918
War Diary	Lobbes	18/12/1918	18/12/1918
War Diary	Chatelineau	19/12/1918	31/12/1918
Heading	War Diary Of 42nd. Div Trench Mortars. R.A. From 1st January 1919 To 31st January 1919. Volume XXII		
War Diary	Chatelineau	01/01/1919	31/01/1919

42ND DIVISION

TRENCH MORTAR BTTS

APR 1917-JAN 1919

Confidential

War Diary of

Z/42

Medium Trench Mortar Battery

From 1st April 1917 To 30 Apr. 1917

VOLUME 1

Instructions regarding War Diaries and Intelligence Summaries are contained in F. S. Regs., Part II. and the Staff Manual respectively. Title pages will be prepared in manuscript.

WAR DIARY

~~or~~

~~INTELLIGENCE SUMMARY.~~ I/42/TMB

(*Erase heading not required.*)

Army Form C. 2118.

Place	Date	Hour	Summary of Events and Information	Remarks and references to Appendices
	1917 APR			
LE PLESSEIL	1		Battery engaged in training having arrived in this Village March 23rd from the 4th Army School of Mortars	JHM
	4		The battery moves to new area by motor Lorry & takes up billets at BOIS OLYMPE, CAPPY (Map Ref: Sheet 62c 1:40.000 G 31 b: France)	JHM
BOIS OLYMPE	21		Battery move by March & motor Lorry to PERONNE (France: Sheet 62c 1:40,000 I 27 b)	JHM
PERONNE	23		One NCO & 6 gunners attached to a/210th Bde RFA	JHM
	30		During the month the battery has been engaged in training and fatigues & ordinary routine	JHM

J Hesketh Capt RGA
D.T.M.O. 42nd Div

T2134. Wt. W708—776. 500000. 4/15. Sir J. C. & S.

Confidential ~

War Diary of Medium T.M. Battery

Y/42

From April 1st 1917 To Apr. 30th 1917

VOLUME 1

Instructions regarding War Diaries and Intelligence Summaries are contained in F. S. Regs., Part II. and the Staff Manual respectively. Title pages will be prepared in manuscript.

WAR DIARY or ~~INTELLIGENCE SUMMARY.~~

(*Erase heading not required.*)

Y/42 T.M.B.

Army Form C. 2118.

Place	Date	Hour	Summary of Events and Information	Remarks and references to Appendices
	1917 Apr			
LE PLESSEIL ABBEVILLE	1		Battery engaged in training having arrived in this village March 23 from SCHOOL OF MORTARS, 4th ARMY.	[illegible]
	4.		Battery moved by motor lorry to BOIS OLYMPE, CAPPY (Map ref. France Sheet 62c 1:40.000 G.31b) + take up billets	[illegible]
Bois OLYMPE	21		Move to Peronne by march + by motor lorry + take up billets there. (Map ref: France: Sheet 62c 1:40,000 I 27b)	[illegible]
	23		One NCO + 6 gunners attached B/210 Bde R.F.A	[illegible]
			During the month the battery has been engaged on Training, fatigues + ordinary Routine	[illegible]

[illegible] Capt R.A.
D.T.M.O. 42 Div

T2134. Wt. W708—776. 500000. 4/15. Sir J. C. & S.

Confidential

War Diary of

X/42

Medium Trench Mortar Battery

From April 1st 1917 To 30 Apr. 1917

VOLUME 1

Instructions regarding War Diaries and Intelligence Summaries are contained in F. S. Regs., Part II. and the Staff Manual respectively. Title pages will be prepared in manuscript.

WAR DIARY

~~or~~

~~INTELLIGENCE SUMMARY.~~ X/42 T.M.B.

(Erase heading not required.)

Army Form C. 2118.

Place	Date	Hour	Summary of Events and Information	Remarks and references to Appendices
	1917 APR			
LE PLESSEIL ABBEVILLE	1		The Battery arrives in this village from the 4th Army School of Mortars on March 23rd, and is engaged in training	[illegible]
"	4		The Battery proceed by motor lorry to BOIS OLYMPE, CAPPY (Map ref. France Sheet 62c 1:40.000 Q31.b) where they take up billets with the brigade	[illegible]
BOIS OLYMPE	21		Move to forward area by march + motor lorry + take up billets at PERONNE. (France Sheet 62c 1:40,000 I27b)	[illegible]
PERONNE	23		One N.C.O. + 6 gunners attached to D/210 Bde + 1 NCO. to 211th Bde RFA	[illegible]
			During the month the battery has been engaged in training, fatigues + ordinary routine.	[illegible]

T2134. Wt. W708—776. 500000. 4/15. Sir J. C. & S.

42

Vol I

Confidential

War Diary of

V/42

Heavy Trench Mortar Battery

From April 1st 1917 to Apr. 30th 1917

VOLUME 1.

Army Form C. 2118.

WAR DIARY

~~or~~

~~INTELLIGENCE SUMMARY.~~ V/42 T.M.B.

(*Erase heading not required.*)

Instructions regarding War Diaries and Intelligence Summaries are contained in F. S. Regs., Part II. and the Staff Manual respectively. Title pages will be prepared in manuscript.

Place	Date	Hour	Summary of Events and Information	Remarks and references to Appendices
	1917 APR.			
LE PLESSEIL ABBEVILLE	1		The battery, billetted in this village since March 23, ~~are~~ is engaged in training having arrived from the 4th Army T. Mortar School on 23rd March	[illegible]
	4		The battery move with the T.M. Brigade to new area by motor lorry & take up billets at BOIS OLYMPE, CAPPY. (Map Ref: Sheet 62c 1:40.000 G 31 b) France.	[illegible]
BOIS OLYMPE	21		The battery move by motor lorry, & by march, to PERONNE (France Sheet 62c 1:40.000 I 27 b)	[illegible]
PERONNE	23	9.30	1 NCO + 26 men attached to 211th Bde R.F.A.	[illegible]
	30		During the month the battery has been engaged on Training, fatigues and ordinary routine.	[illegible]

[illegible] Capt RFA
D.T.M.O. 42nd Div.

T2134. Wt. W708—776. 500000. 4/15. Sir J. C. & S.

Confidential

WAR DIARY Vol. II.
or
~~INTELLIGENCE SUMMARY.~~
(Erase heading not required.)

V/42 T.M.B

Army Form C. 2118.

Instructions regarding War Diaries and Intelligence Summaries are contained in F. S. Regs., Part II. and the Staff Manual respectively. Title pages will be prepared in manuscript.

From May 1st 1917 Summary of Events and Information To May 31st 1917

Place	Date	Hour	Summary of Events and Information	Remarks and references to Appendices
	1917 MAY			
PERONNE	1		Battery (with the exception of 1 N.C.O. + 6 men attached B/210 Bde R.H.A) engaged on fatigues and ordinary routine	Hhh
Map ref. France Sheet 62c 1:40,000 I 27 b	19		Men attached to B/210 Bde R.H.A., above referred to, rejoin battery	Hhh
	20		Battery left for ~~Marquaix~~ MARQUAIX and were attached D/210 Wagon lines + 3rd Brigade R.H.A., 1/Cavalry Division.	Hhh
	21–23rd		Fatigues and ordinary routine, drill etc.	Hhh
	24		Men attached to D/210 for duty, doing the same work as the battery to which attached until 28/5/17.	Hhh
	29		Orders received for the men to do fatigue work at 3rd Brigade R.H.A. H.Q's commencing 30/5/17 and to continue until further notice.	Hhh
	30		These men are in two reliefs: 7.30 am. & 1.30 p.m., the last party returning at 8. p.m. This fatigue employs all the men of the battery	Hhh
	31		Same fatigue continues	Hhh

Vol. II

H. Leslie Hewitt Capt R.A.
D.T.M.O. 42nd Div.

T2134. Wt. W708—776. 500000. 4/15. Sir J. C. & S.

Confidential

WAR DIARY Vol. II

~~or~~

~~INTELLIGENCE SUMMARY.~~

(Erase heading not required.)

Army Form C. 2118.

Instructions regarding War Diaries and Intelligence Summaries are contained in F. S. Regs., Part II. and the Staff Manual respectively. Title pages will be prepared in manuscript.

Z/42 T.M.B.

Place	Date	Hour	Summary of Events and Information — From May 1st 1917 To May 31st 1917	Remarks and references to Appendices
	1917 May			
PERONNE	1		The Battery (with the exception of 6 men attached A210/Bde R.F.A.) at work on fatigues and engaged in ordinary routine	
Map. ref France Sheet 62c 1:40,000 I.27.b			Lieut G. Stephenson, O.C., proceeds to 42/DAC to be temporarily attached	HHh
	11		O.C. returns from D.A.C. and attends instructors' Course at the 4th Army School of Mortars.	HHh
	24		O.C. rejoins Battery.	HHh
	26	10.30 a.m.	Battery moves to new area with Brigade by motor lorry.	
		1 p.m.	Arrival at BERTINCOUT. Battery takes up quarters under Canvas with Brigade. Position on map: Sheet 57c 1:40,000 P.7 d 9.8 (France)	HHh
	27		Party of men engaged building ammunition dump – This fatigue to continue for some days.	HHh
	29		One man detached to join party to assist 2/Lieut J Nicholson (V/42 attached 42/DAC) on Special duty III Corps R.A.	HHh
	30 –	31st	Battery engaged on fatigues & ordinary routine.	HHh

Vol II

HHeskeheivitt Capt RFA
D.A.M.O. 42nd Div Arty

T2134. Wt. W708–776. 500000. 4/15. Sir J. C. & S.

Instructions regarding War Diaries and Intelligence Summaries are contained in F. S. Regs., Part II. and the Staff Manual respectively. Title pages will be prepared in manuscript.

Confidential

WAR DIARY Vol. II

~~or~~

~~INTELLIGENCE SUMMARY.~~ X/42. T.M.B.

(Erase heading not required.)

Army Form C. 2118.

From May 1st 1917 — To May 31st 1917

Place	Date	Hour	Summary of Events and Information	Remarks and references to Appendices
	1917 May			
PERONNE (Map ref France Sheet 62c 1:40,000 I.27.b)	1		The Battery (with the exception of 7 men attached to D/210 Bde R.F.A. & one man attached to 211/Bde R.F.A.) engaged in fatigues and ordinary Routine	[initials]
	11		The Battery complete with guns proceeds to the 4th Army School of Mortars, VAUX-EN-AMIENOIS to attend the 13th Course	[initials]
VAUX-EN-AMIENOIS	12		Report to Commandant of School	[initials]
	23		Course disperses	[initials]
	24		Battery re-joins 42nd Division Trench Mortar Brigade at PERONNE	[initials]
PERONNE	26	a.m. 10.30	Battery moves to new area with Brigade by motor lorry	
	"	1.pm	Arrival at BERTINCOURT. Battery takes up quarters under canvas; Position of Camp on map: France Sheet 57c 1:40,000 P7d9.8	[initials]
	27th		Party of men detailed to build ammunition dump; this fatigue to continue for some days	[initials]
	29th		Two men detached to assist 2/Lieut. Nicholson V/42 attached 42/DAC on Special duty III Corps R.A.	[initials]
	30–31		Fatigues & Ordinary Routine	[initials]

Vol. II

[signature] Capt R.F.A. D.211.O. [illegible]

T2134. Wt. W708–776. 500000. 4/15. Sir J. C. & S.

Confidential

Instructions regarding War Diaries and Intelligence Summaries are contained in F. S. Regs., Part II. and the Staff Manual respectively. Title pages will be prepared in manuscript.

WAR DIARY Vol II
or
~~INTELLIGENCE SUMMARY.~~
(Erase heading not required.)

Army Form C. 2118.

Y/42 T.M.B.

From May 1st 1917 to May 31st 1917

Place	Date	Hour	Summary of Events and Information	Remarks and references to Appendices
PERONNE (Map ref: France Sheet 62.C. 1:40.000 I.27b	1917 May 1		The Battery (with the exception of 27 men attached to 211th Brigade R.F.A.) engaged on fatigues and ordinary routine.	
			2/Lieut T. Nicholson, Right half Section Commander attached to 42/D.A.C.	A.H.L.
	12		2/Lieut S. F. Hayward, Left half Section Commander attached to 42/D.A.C	A.H.L.
	24		Captain A. Pringle Livingstone, Battery Commander proceeds to the 4th Army School of Mortars to attend Course of instruction in D.T.M.O's duties.	A.H.L.
	26	a.m. 10.30	Battery moves with Brigade to new Area by motor Lorry	A.H.L.
		1.pm	Arrival at BERTINCOURT. The Brigade take up quarters under Canvas. Exact position of Camp on Map: France, Sheet 57c 1:40,000 P.7.d 9.8	A.H.L.
BERTINCOURT	27		Party of men detailed for building ammunition dump - This fatigue to continue for some days	A.H.L.
	28		2/Lieut Nicholson (attached D.A.C) detailed for Special duty 3rd Corps R.A. one man from this battery proceeds with a party from the brigade to assist in this work -	A.H.L.
	29th - 31st		The Battery engaged on fatigues and ordinary routine	A.H.L.

Vol. II

A.H. Leslie Hewitt Capt R.F.A. D.T.M.O. 42nd Div

T2134. Wt. W708—776. 500000. 4/15. Sir J. C. & S.

Instructions regarding War Diaries and Intelligence Summaries are contained in F. S. Regs., Part II. and the Staff Manual respectively. Title pages will be prepared in manuscript.

WAR DIARY "Z 42" TRENCH MORTAR BATTERY.
or
~~INTELLIGENCE SUMMARY.~~
(Erase heading not required.)

Army Form C. 2118.

Place	Date	Hour	Summary of Events and Information	Remarks and references to Appendices
			VOL. 3	
BERTINCOURT. P7.d.9.8 France Sheet 57C.	1st-6 1917 to 4th		General fatigues and improvement of Camp.	[illegible]
— " —	5th		6 O.R's rejoin Battery from 210 Bde, Wagon Lines, YTRES. O24. D.6.8. Sheet 57C.	
— " —	6th		Medium Trench Mortar (2") Emplacements commenced at Q3.b. Central Q3.b 4½. 2½ + Q3.a. 7. 7½	
— " —	9th		Battery & Personnel proceed to New Area, HAVRINGCOURT WOOD. P18. b18 Sheet 57C	[illegible]
HAVRINGCOURT WOOD. P18. b18 France Sheet 57C	10th to 22nd		Work on Emplacements and dug-outs at above position continued	
— " —	23rd		Three rounds (2") fired on enemy Barricade at K33. C88. Sheet 57C.	
— " —	24th to 28th		Work on Emplacements and dug-out continued.	[illegible]
— " —	29th		One round (2") fired } at SHROPSHIRE SPUR. K33. D.9.3 from Q3. b. central	
— " —	30th		Nine rounds (2") fired }	

[illegible] Capt RFA
D.T.M.O. 42nd Div A.S.

T2134. Wt. W708—776. 500000. 4/15. Sir J. C. & S.

Instructions regarding War Diaries and Intelligence Summaries are contained in F. S. Regs., Part II. and the Staff Manual respectively. Title pages will be prepared in manuscript.

WAR DIARY "Y42" Trench Mortar Battery. Army Form C. 2118.

or

INTELLIGENCE ~~SUMMARY~~.

(Erase heading not required.)

Place	Date	Hour	Summary of Events and Information	Remarks and references to Appendices
			VOL. 3.	
MARQUAIX	1/6/17 to 7th		General fatigue with 2nd Cavalry Division.	
—"—	8th		Battery rejoins Brigade at BERTINCOURT. P7.d 9.8. Sheet 57.C.	
BERTINCOURT. P7.d 9.8. France Sheet 57C.	9th	10AM	Battery & Personnel proceed to new Area, HAVRINGCOURT WOOD. P18. b1.8 Sheet 57 C.	
HAVRINGCOURT WOOD. France Sheet 57C.	10th to 18th		Supplying working parties for Emplacements for "X and Z 42" Batteries. at K32.a.8.5. K32.a.9.6. Q3.b Central. Q.3.b 4½.2½. & Q 3.a 7.7½.	
—"—	19th	10AM	Battery proceeds to 4th Army School of Mortars, VAUX-EN-AMIENS, for course of Instructions.	
VAUX-EN-AMIENS.	21st to 30th		Drill and Instruction at 4th Army School of Mortars.	

Blackwell Capt RFA
D.T.M.O. 42nd Div Art.

T2134. Wt. W708—776. 500000. 4/15. Sir J. C. & S.

Instructions regarding War Diaries and Intelligence Summaries are contained in F. S. Regs., Part II. and the Staff Manual respectively. Title pages will be prepared in manuscript.

WAR DIARY "X 42" Trench Mortar Battery.
or
~~INTELLIGENCE SUMMARY.~~
(Erase heading not required.)

Army Form C. 2118.

Place	Date	Hour	Summary of Events and Information	Remarks and references to Appendices
			VOL. 3.	
BERTINCOURT. P7.D9.8. France sheet 57.C.	1.6.1917.		General fatigues and Improvement of Camp.	
—"—	6th		Medium T.M. (2") Emplacements commenced at K.32.a.8.5 & K32.a.9.6.	
—"—	9th	10AM	Battery & Personnel remove to HAVRINGCOURT WOOD P18.b1.8. Sheet 57C.	
HAVRINGCOURT WOOD Sheet 57.C.	10th		1 Officer & 1 O.R. rejoin from 4th Army T.M. School VAUX-EN-AMIENS.	
	10th		2 O.R's rejoin from Divisional Signal School. Bus. O24. Sheet 57 C.	
—"— —"—	10th to 30th		Work on Emplacements and dug-outs continued at K32.a.8.5 & K32.a.9.6.	

H. [illegible] Capt R.F.A.
D.T.M.O. 42nd Divl Arty

T2134. Wt. W708—776. 500000. 4/15. Sir J. C. & S.

Instructions regarding War Diaries and Intelligence Summaries are contained in F. S. Regs., Part II. and the Staff Manual respectively. Title pages will be prepared in manuscript.

WAR DIARY or ~~INTELLIGENCE SUMMARY.~~ V 42 TRENCH MORTAR BATTERY.

(Erase heading not required.)

Army Form C. 2118.

VOL. 3

Place	Date	Hour	Summary of Events and Information	Remarks and references to Appendices
BERTINCOURT P.7.D.9.8. SHEET 57.C	1st 6. 1917.		General fatigues and improvement of Camp.	
— " —	5th		25 O.R's rejoined Battery from 211 Bde, Wagon Lines YTRES. O.24. D6.8. Sheet 57C.	
— " —	6th 6.17.	9AM	1 Officer & 22 O.R's proceed to T.M. School at VAUX-EN-AMIENS.	
— " —	"	8.30AM.	1 N.C.O & 10 men commence to make 9.45" Trench Howitzer emplacement at	K 32. a 2 4 Sheet 57C.
— " —	7.6.17 8.6.17		Work on emplacement continued & dugout commenced.	
— " —	9.6.17	10AM	Battery & Personnel proceed to New Quarters at HAVRINCOURT WOOD P18.B1.8. Sheet 57C.	
HAVRINGCOURT WOOD P18.b1.8. FRANCE SHEET 57C	10th to 15th		Work on emplacement & dug-out continued.	
— " —	16th	10.10AM to 11-30	Fired eleven rounds (9.45") and obtained three direct hits on K27. C.0.8 and four direct hits on K27. C2.8. Sheet 57C.	
— " —	17th	9AM	2 O.R's proceed, for course of Instruction, to Divisional Signal School Bus O.24 Sheet 57C.	
	19th		1 Officer & 22 O.R's rejoin Battery from T.M. school VAUX-EN-AMIENS.	

Continued —

[illegible] Capt RA
D.T.M.O. 42nd Div.

T2134. Wt. W708—776. 500000. 4/15. Sir J. C. & S.

Instructions regarding War Diaries and Intelligence Summaries are contained in F. S. Regs., Part II. and the Staff Manual respectively. Title pages will be prepared in manuscript.

WAR DIARY V42 T.M.B. Continued.
or
~~INTELLIGENCE SUMMARY.~~
(Erase heading not required.)

Army Form C. 2118.

Place	Date	Hour	Summary of Events and Information	Remarks and references to Appendices
			Vol. 3.	
HAVRINCOURT WOOD. P18.b.1.8. France Sheet 57C.	17th 6.1917 to 29th		Improving Emplacement & dug-out for permanent use.	
— " —	29th	8 P.M.	New position marked out for Heavy Trench Mortar ~~at~~	
— " —	30th	9 AM	New Emplacement commenced at Q3.b.6.8 and work on position at K32.a.2.4 continued.	
			Hheslehurst Capt RFA D.T.M.O. 42nd Div Art	

T2134. Wt. W708—776. 500000. 4/15. Sir J. C. & S.

Instructions regarding War Diaries and Intelligence Summaries are contained in F. S. Regs., Part II. and the Staff Manual respectively. Title pages will be prepared in manuscript.

WAR DIARY 242 TRENCH MORTAR BATTERY.
or
~~INTELLIGENCE SUMMARY.~~
(Erase heading not required.)

Army Form C. 2118.

JULY 1917. SHEET 1

Place	Date	Hour	Summary of Events and Information	Remarks and references to Appendices
	July 1917.		REFERENCES MAP. 1/20.000 57c. VOL IV	
HAVRINCOURT WOOD P18 b. 1.8 France sheet 57.C.	1st	10.30 PM to 11.15 PM	10 rounds 2" bombs were fired by allied T.M. from Q3. b. central on ELEPHANT SHELTERS K33. d. 8 15. at request of Infantry. Slight retaliation by hostile T.M's.	HHh
	2nd	10.30 PM	4 rounds 2" bombs fired by allied T.M's from Q3. b. central, on K33. d. 6.4	HHh
	3rd	2.30 AM	6 - - - - - - - - - - - - -	
	3rd	10.15 PM to 11.15 PM	12 - - - - - - - - - - - - on SHROPSHIRE SPUR K33. d. 8 3.	
	night 4/5th		10 rounds 2" bombs fired by allied T.M. on K33 d. 4 5 & vicinity.	
	7th		61 - - - - - - - - on SHROPSHIRE SPUR between K33 d & K34 C.	HHh
	8 to 17th		Working Parties on emplacement & dugouts.	HHh
	18th	2 AM	4 rounds 2" bombs fired on SHROPSHIRE SPUR – ELEPHANT HUTS + MOW COP. –	HHh
	19 20		Working Parties	HHh
	21		4 rounds 2" bombs fired on DEAN COPSE.	
	22		4 - - - - on MOW COP at request of Infantry.	HHh

Continued –

T2134. Wt. W708–776. 500000. 4/15. Sir J. C. & S.

Instructions regarding War Diaries and Intelligence Summaries are contained in F. S. Regs., Part II. and the Staff Manual respectively. Title pages will be prepared in manuscript.

WAR DIARY or INTELLIGENCE SUMMARY.

(*Erase heading not required.*)

Z 42 TRENCH MORTAR BATTERY

Army Form C. 2118.

SHEET 2.

Place	Date	Hour	Summary of Events and Information	Remarks and references to Appendices
	JULY 1917		VOL IV Continued:-	
HAVRINCOURT WOOD P18. b.1.8 France Sheet 57 C.	23rd to 31.		Working Parties on Emplacements adjoints.	[illegible]
			[illegible] Capt R.F.A. DTMO. 42 Div Arty.	

T2134. Wt. W708–776. 500000. 4/15. Sir J. C. & S.

Instructions regarding War Diaries and Intelligence Summaries are contained in F. S. Regs., Part II. and the Staff Manual respectively. Title pages will be prepared in manuscript.

WAR DIARY Y 42 TRENCH MORTAR BATTERY
or
INTELLIGENCE SUMMARY.
(Erase heading not required.)

Army Form C. 2118.

SHEET 1

Place	Date	Hour	Summary of Events and Information	Remarks and references to Appendices
	July 1917.		REFERENCES MAP FRANCE 1/20.000 57c VOL IV	
VAUX-ETN-AMIENS	1st to 3rd		Lt Horn & 21 O.R's attached IV Army School of Mortars, VAUX-EN-AMIENS.	[initials]
	4th		Lt Horn & 21 ORs return to Brigade from IV Army School of Mortars.	[initials]
HAVRINCOURT WOOD P.18.b.1.8 France sheet 57C.	5th to 11th night		Working Parties on gun emplacement & dugout.	[initials]
	11/12th	12.7AM to 12.37	31 rounds 2" bombs fired by Med: TM on DEAN COPSE & ETNA.	[initials]
	13th to 16th		Working parties on gun emplacement & dugout.	[initials]
	17th	4PM	25 rounds 2" bombs fired by Med TM on WIGAN COPSE	[initials]
	18th to 29th		Working parties on gun emplacement & dugout.	[initials]
	30th		12 rounds 2" bombs fired by Med T.M's on Working Party – enemy dispersed –	[initials]
	31st		New Medium Trench Mortar position commenced at K32.A.7.7½.	

[signature]
Capt R.F.A.
DTMO 42/Div Arty.

T2134. Wt. W708—776. 500000. 4/15. Sir J. C. & S.

Instructions regarding War Diaries and Intelligence Summaries are contained in F. S. Regs., Part II. and the Staff Manual respectively. Title pages will be prepared in manuscript.

WAR DIARY X 42 TRENCH MORTAR BATTERY

~~or~~

~~INTELLIGENCE SUMMARY.~~

(Erase heading not required.)

Army Form C. 2118.

SHEET 1

Place	Date	Hour	Summary of Events and Information	Remarks and references to Appendices
	JULY 1917.		REFERENCES MAP FRANCE 1/20.000 57c VOL IV	
HAVRINCOURT WOOD. P18. b.1.8	1st to 4th		Improving & strengthening emplacement & dugouts at K32 A85 & K32 A9.6.	Ahh
FRANCE SHEET 57C.	5th 6th	11PM to 12.15AM.	Fourteen rounds 2" bombs fired by Medium T.M's between K32.b88 & K26D9.1	
			Twenty - - - - - - - - on K32 b.80.75.	Ahh
	7 to 14th		Working parties on emplacement & dugouts.	Ahh
	midnight 15/16th.		Twentyfive rounds 2" bombs fired by Med: T.Ms on WIGAN COPSE	Ahh
	17th to 19th		Working parties on emplacement & dugouts.	Ahh
	20th.		Six rounds 2" bombs fired in response to S.O.S. Signals.	Ahh
	21st.		Fifteen - - - - - on DEAN COPSE	Ahh
	22	3 to 4PM	Ten rounds 2" bombs fired on DEAN COPSE in conjunction with Heavy T.M's.	Ahh
	23rd	Noon	Four rounds 2" bombs fired by Med: T.M. on WIGAN COPSE	Ahh
			Continued :-	

T2134. Wt. W708–776. 500000. 4/15. Sir J. C. & S.

Instructions regarding War Diaries and Intelligence Summaries are contained in F. S. Regs., Part II. and the Staff Manual respectively. Title pages will be prepared in manuscript.

WAR DIARY X42 T.M.B.

or

~~**INTELLIGENCE SUMMARY.**~~

(Erase heading not required.)

Army Form C. 2118.

SHEET 2

Place	Date	Hour	Summary of Events and Information	Remarks and references to Appendices
			VOL IV Continued.	
HAVRINCOURT WOOD P18.b.1.8 France Sheet 57.C.	23rd	11.10 PM to 11.30 PM.	Twenty round 2" bombs fired on DEAN COPSE in cooperation with the Artillery during raid by our Infantry.	[initials]
	24th to 28th		Working Parties on emplacements & dugouts.	[initials]
	29th		Six rounds 2" bombs fired by X Med. T.M. - registration on WIGAN COPSE	
	30th to 31st		Working Parties on emplacements & dugouts.	[initials]

[signature]
Capt R.F.A.
D.T.M.O.
42 Div Arty

T2134. Wt. W708–776. 500000. 4/15. Sir J. C. & S.

Instructions regarding War Diaries and Intelligence Summaries are contained in F. S. Regs., Part II. and the Staff Manual respectively. Title pages will be prepared in manuscript.

WAR DIARY V42 TRENCH MORTAR BATTERY. or INTELLIGENCE SUMMARY.

(Erase heading not required.)

Army Form C. 2118.

JULY 1917.

SHEET 1.

Place	Date	Hour	Summary of Events and Information	Remarks and references to Appendices
	July 1917.		REFERENCES MAP FRANCE 1/20.000. SHEET 57 c. VOL. IV.	
HAVRINCOURT WOOD. P18 b.1.8	1st 2nd		Work on gun emplacements & dugouts continued at K32.A2.4 (Left gun) & Q3. b 2½.3. (Right gun).	HHh
FRANCE SHEET 57C.	2nd	9AM to 2PM.	Enemy shelled P.18. b.1.8 & HAVRINCOURT WOOD at northern edge of our camp, with about 150 shells 5.9" & 50 – 4.2" H.E.	HHh
	3rd	1.8AM to 1.22AM	Five rounds 9.45" bombs fired by Heavy T.M. from K32. A2.4 on VESUVIUS.	HHh
	4th		1 Officer & 5 O.R's rejoin from 35 Div: R.A.	HHh
			2nd Heavy Trench Mortar put in at Q3. b. 2½. 3.	HHh
	"	5.34 to 6.4 PM	Seven rounds 9.45" bombs fired by H.T.M. from K32. A 2.4 on Road Junction N W of DEAN COPSE	HHh
	5th 6th	11.PM to 12.15AM	Fifteen rounds 9.45" bombs fired by HTM. from K32. A. 2.4 on DEAN COPSE K32. b 80.75.	HHh
	6th	4/6 PM	Twenty rounds 9.45" bombs fired by H.T.M. from Q3. b. 2½. 3. on BOGGARTS HOLE & vicinity.	HHh
	7th to 11th		Work on emplacement & dugouts – repairs & improvement etc.	HHh

Continued –

T2134. Wt. W708–776. 500000. 4/15. Sir J. C. & S.

Instructions regarding War Diaries and Intelligence Summaries are contained in F. S. Regs., Part II. and the Staff Manual respectively. Title pages will be prepared in manuscript.

WAR DIARY V42 TMB.
or
~~INTELLIGENCE SUMMARY.~~
(Erase heading not required.)

Army Form C. 2118.

Continued. SHEET 2

Place	Date	Hour	Summary of Events and Information	Remarks and references to Appendices
	July 1917.		VOL IV Continued.	
HAVRINCOURT WOOD	12th	12.7 to 12.37 AM.	Ten rounds 9.45" bombs fired by H.T.M. from Q3. b 2½. 3 on ~~Dean Copse~~ BOGGARTS HOLE	[illegible]
P.18 b.1.8 France Sheet 57C.	13th	5.10 PM to 5.40 PM.	Six rounds 9.45" " " " " " K32. A.2.4 on SUNKEN ROAD & VESUVIUS.	[illegible]
	14th		Working parties on positions	[illegible]
	15th		Two rounds 9.45" bombs fired by H.T.M. from K32 A.2.4 registration on SUNKEN ROAD & VESUVIUS.	[illegible]
	16th	10.3 PM to 10.33 PM.	Eleven rounds 9.45" bombs fired - - - Q3. b. 2½. 3. on BOGGARTS HOLE.	[illegible]
	17th	4 PM	Two rounds 9.45" - - - - - K32. A.2.4 registration on WIGAN COPSE.	[illegible]
	18th to 20th		Working parties on positions.	[illegible]
	21st		Six rounds 9.45" bombs fired by H.T.M. from Q3. b. 2½. 3 on ~~Dean~~ Copse K.33. d. 9½ 9½ (Suspected Hostile T.M. Position)	[illegible]
			Continued.	

T2134. Wt. W708—776. 500000. 4/15. Sir J. C. & S.

Instructions regarding War Diaries and Intelligence Summaries are contained in F. S. Regs., Part II. and the Staff Manual respectively. Title pages will be prepared in manuscript.

WAR DIARY V42 T.M.B.
or
~~INTELLIGENCE SUMMARY.~~
(Erase heading not required.)

Army Form C. 2118.

SHEET 3.

Place	Date	Hour	Summary of Events and Information	Remarks and references to Appendices
			VOL IV Continued.	
HAVRINCOURT WOOD. P18. b 1 8 France Sheet 57 C.	22nd	3 PM to 4 PM	Twenty rounds 9.45" bombs fired by H.T.M. from Q3. b. 2½. 3. – concentrated bombardment – on DEAN COPSE. DEAN COPSE now almost completely destroyed.	[illegible]
	–	10.30 to 10.33 PM.	Two rounds 9.45" bombs fired by H.T.M. from ~~Q3. b. 2½. 3~~ K.32. a. 2. 4 on DEAN COPSE in cooperation with the Artillery in a three minutes preparation, previous to Inf. attack	[illegible]
	23	Noon	Fourteen rounds 9.45" bombs fired by H.T.M. from Q3 b 2½. 3 on suspected hostile Medium T.M. position at K33. b. 9½. 9½.	
	–	11.10 PM to 11.30 PM.	Ten rounds 9.45" bombs fired by H.T.M. from K32 A 2.4 on DEAN COPSE in cooperation with the Artillery, during raid by our Infantry. To create diversion the H.T.M. at Q3. b. 2½. 3 fired [illegible] rounds 9.45" bombs on suspected hostile Medium T.M. position K.33. b. 7. 7 at the same time. Our 2" TM's also fired during this operation.	[illegible]
	24 to 29		Working parties on emplacement.	
	30th (3rd) 31st		New Heavy Mortar position commenced at K32. A 4½. 3. Working parties on emplacement.	[illegible]

[signature]
Capt R.F.A.
D.T.M.O. 42 Div Arty.

T2134. Wt. W708—776. 500000. 4/15. Sir J. C. & S.

Instructions regarding War Diaries and Intelligence Summaries are contained in F. S. Regs., Part II. and the Staff Manual respectively. Title pages will be prepared in manuscript.

WAR DIARY or ~~INTELLIGENCE SUMMARY.~~ Z 42 TRENCH MORTAR BATTERY

(Erase heading not required.)

Army Form C. 2118.

AUGUST 1917.

Place	Date	Hour	Summary of Events and Information	Remarks and references to Appendices
	AUGUST 1917.		VOL V.	
HAVRINCOURT WOOD. P18 F.1.8 France Sheet 57C	1st	9 P.M.	7 rounds 2" bombs were fired by Medium trench mortars on new barbed wire K32. b. 5.7.	[illegible]
	2nd to 15th		General fatigues in the line.	
	16th		All Medium positions - HAVRINCOURT SECTOR - handed over to the 9th DIVISION. HERMIES SECTOR taken over from the 9th DIVISION TRENCH MORTARS.	[illegible]
	17th to 20th		General fatigues in the line.	
	20th		Proceed with the Brigade to Nr Bus O.24. 8.3. Sheet 57C SW. for rest.	[illegible]
BUS O.24 8.3. Sheet 57C.	25th		Proceed by Motor lorries to BAPAUME	
BAPAUME	26th		Entrain for PROVEN.	
PROVEN	27th		Arrive PROVEN & proceed by Motor lorries to WATOU K9. C 8.5. Sheet 27.	
WATOU. K9. C. 8.5 Sheet 27.	29th		Proceed by Motor lorries to VLAMERTINGHE H7 C 3.4. Sheet 28.	[illegible]
VLAMERTINGHE H7. C. 3.4 Sheet 28.	30th to 31st		Fatigues on R.A. Ammunition Dumps.	

[signature] Capt R.F.A. D.T.M.O. 42 Div Arty.

T2134. Wt. W708—776. 500000. 4/15. Sir J. C. & S.

Instructions regarding War Diaries and Intelligence Summaries are contained in F. S. Regs., Part II. and the Staff Manual respectively. Title pages will be prepared in manuscript.

WAR DIARY Y/42. TRENCH MORTAR BATTERY.
or
~~INTELLIGENCE SUMMARY.~~
(Erase heading not required.)

AUGUST 1917.

Army Form C. 2118.

Place	Date	Hour	Summary of Events and Information	Remarks and references to Appendices
	AUGUST 1917.		VOL. V.	
HAVRINCOURT WOOD. P15 b.1.8. France Sheet 57C.	1st	3.45AM.	8 rounds 2" bombs were fired by allied T.M. on WIGAN COPSE, at request of Infantry.	J.H.L.
		2.45PM.	8 rounds 2" bombs were fired by allied TM on new barbed wire K26. b 5.7.	J.H.L.
	2nd to 14th		General fatigues in the line.	
	15th	12 noon.	20 rounds 2" bombs were fired on WIGAN COPSE from K32 A 8.5	
			11 - - - - - - ETNA -	J.H.L.
	-	3 PM	11 - - - - - WIGAN COPSE -	
	16th		All medium positions HAVRINCOURT SECTOR - handed over to the 9th DIVISION	
	16th		HERMIES SECTOR taken over from the 9th DIVISION TRENCH MORTARS.	J.H.L.
	17th to 20th		General fatigues in the line.	
	20th		Proceed with the Brigade to New Area. Bus O24. 8.3 Sheet 57c SW for rest.	
Bus O24. 8.3 Sheet 57 C	25th		Proceed by motor lorries to ~~BALLEAUTRE~~ BAPAUME	J.H.L.
			Continued -	

T2134. Wt. W708—776. 500000. 4/15. Sir J. C. & S.

Instructions regarding War Diaries and Intelligence Summaries are contained in F. S. Regs., Part II. and the Staff Manual respectively. Title pages will be prepared in manuscript.

WAR DIARY
or
~~INTELLIGENCE SUMMARY.~~
(Erase heading not required.)

Y/42 TRENCH MORTAR BATTERY.
AUGUST 1917.

Army Form C. 2118.

Place	Date	Hour	Summary of Events and Information	Remarks and references to Appendices
			VOL. V. Continued:-	
BAUPAUME	26th		Entrain for PROVEN.	
PROVEN.	27th		Arrive PROVEN & proceed by Motor lorries to WATOU K9.C 8.5 Sheet 27	
WATOU K9.C 8.5. Sheet 27.	29th		Proceed by Motor lorries to VLAMERTINGHE H7.C.3.4. Sheet 28.	
VLAMERTINGHE H7.C.3.4. Sheet 28.	30th to 31st		Fatigues on RA Ammunition Dumps.	

[signature]
Capt R.F.A.
D.T.M.O.
42/ Div Arty

T2134. Wt. W708—776. 500000. 4/15. Sir J. C. & S.

Army Form C. 2118.

Instructions regarding War Diaries and Intelligence Summaries are contained in F. S. Regs., Part II. and the Staff Manual respectively. Title pages will be prepared in manuscript.

WAR DIARY "X42" TRENCH MORTAR BATTERY.
or
~~INTELLIGENCE SUMMARY.~~
(Erase heading not required.)

AUGUST 1917.

Place	Date	Hour	Summary of Events and Information	Remarks and references to Appendices
	AUGUST 1917		VOL V	
HAVRINCOURT WOOD	1st – 11th		General fatigues in the line.	
P18.6.1.8 France Sheet 57C.	12th	1 AM.	14 rounds 2" bombs were fired by Medium Trench Mortars on ETNA	[initials]
		1 PM	26 - - - - - - - - - on Barbed wire WIGAN COPSE	
	13th	2 45 PM.	33 rounds 2" bombs were fired by M T M. on WIGAN COPSE. A number of Germans rushed from the Copse towards their own trench K26 d.4.9. Our Lewis gunners & rifles immediately opened fire on them – killing or wounding 14. The 2" bombs also caused a considerable number of casualties. Large gaps were made in the wire & hostile works destroyed.	[initials]
	16th		All Medium positions – HAVRINCOURT SECTOR – handed over to the 9th DIVISION.	[initials]
	16th		HERMIES SECTOR taken over from the 9th DIVISION TRENCH MORTARS	
	17th – 20th		General fatigues on gun positions K26 C 8½ 9½ & K26 A 7½. ½.	[initials]

Continued. –

T2134. Wt. W708–776. 500000. 4/15. Sir J. C. & S.

Instructions regarding War Diaries and Intelligence Summaries are contained in F. S. Regs., Part II. and the Staff Manual respectively. Title pages will be prepared in manuscript.

WAR DIARY 'X42' TRENCH MORTAR BATTERY
or
~~INTELLIGENCE SUMMARY.~~
(Erase heading not required.)

Army Form C. 2118.

AUGUST 1917.

Place	Date	Hour	Summary of Events and Information	Remarks and references to Appendices
	AUGUST 1917		VOL. V Continued :-	
HAVRINCOURT WOOD P18.6.1.8 France Sheet 57C	20th		Proceed with Brigade to New Area Bus O24. 8 3. Sheet 57 C SW for rest	HhH
Bus. O24 A8 3. France Sheet 57C	25th		Proceed by Motor Lorries to ~~BAUPAUME~~ BAPAUME	HhH
BAUPAUME	26th		Entrain for PROVEN.	
PROVEN	27th		Arrive at PROVEN & proceed by Motor lorries to WATOU K9 C 8.5.	HhH
WATOU K9. C 8.5 Sheet 27.	29th		Proceed by Motor lorries to VLAMERTINGHE H7. C 3.4. Sheet 28.	HhH
VLAMERTINGHE H7. C 3.4 Sheet 28.	30th 31st		Fatigues on R.A. Ammunition Dumps.	HhH

H Heslehurst
Capt RFA
D.T.M.O.
42/ Div Arty

T2134. Wt. W708—776. 500000. 4/15. Sir J. C. & S.

Instructions regarding War Diaries and Intelligence Summaries are contained in F. S. Regs., Part II. and the Staff Manual respectively. Title pages will be prepared in manuscript.

WAR DIARY
or
~~INTELLIGENCE SUMMARY.~~
(Erase heading not required.)

V42 TRENCH MORTAR BATTERY.

AUGUST 1917.

Army Form C. 2118.

Place	Date	Hour	Summary of Events and Information	Remarks and references to Appendices
	August 1917		VOL V.	
HAVRINCOURT WOOD. P18. b.1.8 France Sheet 57C.	4th	2 PM.	14 rounds 9.45" bombs were fired by Heavy Trench Mortar from K32. A 2.4 on SUNKEN ROAD & RIFLE PITS N.W. of WIGAN COPSE, sweeping Westward from the Eastern end of SUNKEN ROAD. Six direct hits were obtained on the road & a short round scored a direct hit on Enemy's New Trench K27. C2.3. Enemy artillery retaliated for 3/4 hour with 4.2's, searching YORKSHIRE BANK in vicinity of Heavy T.M. position.	[illegible]
	6th	6 to 8 PM.	15 rounds 9.45" bombs were fired by H.T.M from Q3. b. 2½ 3 on BOGGARTS HOLE. 9 direct hits were obtained. Eleven rounds 9.45" were fired by Heavy TM on Enemy T.M. which had opened in retaliation. 6 rounds fell in close vicinity of hostile TM which ceased firing	[illegible]
	16th		7 rounds 9.45" were fired from K32. A. 2.4 on WIGAN COPSE Two Heavy Trench Mortars & all positions taken over by the 9th Div Trench Mortars.	[illegible]

T2131. Wt. W708—776. 500000. 4/15. Sir J. C. & S.

Continued.

Instructions regarding War Diaries and Intelligence Summaries are contained in F. S. Regs., Part II. and the Staff Manual respectively. Title pages will be prepared in manuscript.

WAR DIARY V42 TRENCH MORTAR BATTERY.
or
INTELLIGENCE SUMMARY.
(Erase heading not required.)

Army Form C. 2118.

Place	Date	Hour	Summary of Events and Information	Remarks and references to Appendices
	AUGUST	1917	VOL V Continued	
HAVRINCOURT WOOD.	16th		HERMIES SECTOR taken over from 9th Div TRENCH MORTARS. One Heavy T.M. - - - - - -	JHh
I18. c.1.8 France Sheet 57c.	16th to 19th		Working parties building Heavy T.M. position at HERMIES.	
	20th		One Heavy TM & position handed over to 9th Div TRENCH MORTARS. (HERMIES)	
	20th		The Brigade move to New Area BUS O.24. A.8.3 - Sheet 57c - SW. for rest.	JHh
BUS O.24. A 8.3.	25th		The Brigade proceed by Motor Lorries to ~~BAPAUME~~ BAPAUME	
BAUPAUME	26th		The Brigade entrain for PROVEN.	
PROVEN	27th		Arrive at PROVEN & proceed by motor lorries to WATOU K9. C 8.5. Ref Sheet 27.	
WATOU K9. C. 8.5. Sheet 27.	29th		The Brigade proceed by motor lorries to VLAMERTINGHE H7. C 3.4 Sheet 28.	JHh
	29th		Heavy Trench Mortar taken over from 15th DIVISION TM's at C.30 Central	
VLAMERTINGHE Sheet 28.	30th to 31st		Working parties at position at GREY RUIN C.30 Central & R.A. Ammunition Dumps	
			[signature] Capt RFA D.T.M.O. 42/Div Arty	

T2134. Wt. W708—776. 500000. 4/15. Sir J. C. & S.

Instructions regarding War Diaries and Intelligence Summaries are contained in F. S. Regs., Part II. and the Staff Manual respectively. Title pages will be prepared in manuscript.

WAR DIARY Z42 TRENCH MORTAR BATTERY.
or
~~INTELLIGENCE SUMMARY~~. SEPTEMBER 1917.
(Erase heading not required.)

Army Form C. 2118.

Place	Date	Hour	Summary of Events and Information	Remarks and references to Appendices
	SEPT 1917.			
VLAMERTINGHE	1st		Fatigues in the line & on RA. Ammunition Dumps.	
H 8c7.6.	5			
SHEET 28.	12th			[initials]
	13th		E.A. dropped bombs in vicinity of camp. 1 Sergeant severely wounded. 6" gun emplacement destroyed by shell fire - 4 OR's wounded when bringing gun from position - 1 since died of wounds -	[initials]
	14th		12 OR's attached VANCOUVER DUMP. H8. D73 for fatigues.	[initials]
	19th		1 Officer & .3 OR's attached 210th Bde R.F.A.	
	29th		1 Officer & 14 OR's return from VANCOUVER DUMP & 210th Bde RFA.	
	30th		Proceed by motor lorries to WORMHOUT - arrive WORMHOUT & in camp for the night.	[initials]

H. Hewitt
Capt RFA
D.T.M.O.
47 Div Arty

T2134. Wt. W708—776. 500000. 4/15. Sir J. C. & S.

Instructions regarding War Diaries and Intelligence Summaries are contained in F. S. Regs., Part II. and the Staff Manual respectively. Title pages will be prepared in manuscript.

WAR DIARY Y42. TRENCH MORTAR. BATTERY.
or
~~INTELLIGENCE SUMMARY.~~ SEPTEMBER. 1917.
(Erase heading not required.)

Army Form C. 2118.

Place	Date	Hour	Summary of Events and Information	Remarks and references to Appendices
	SEPT 1917.			
VLAMERTINGHE	1st		Fatigues in the line & on R.A. Ammunition Dumps.	[initials]
H8.c.7.6	to			
SHEET 28.	18th			
	19th		4 N.C.O's & 14 gunners attached 211 Bde. R.F.A.	
	29th		3 N.C.O's & 13 gunners return from 211 Bde. R.F.A.	
	30th		Proceed by motor lorries for WORMHOUT en route for COXYDE Bain	[initials]
	30th		Arrive WORMHOUT & encamp for the night.	

[signature]
Capt R.F.A.
D.T.M.O.
42 Div Arty

T2134. Wt. W708-776. 500000. 4/15. Sir J. C. & S.

Instructions regarding War Diaries and Intelligence Summaries are contained in F. S. Regs., Part II. and the Staff Manual respectively. Title pages will be prepared in manuscript.

WAR DIARY "X42" TRENCH MORTAR BATTERY. or ~~INTELLIGENCE SUMMARY~~.

(Erase heading not required.)

Army Form C. 2118.

SEPTEMBER 1917.

Place	Date	Hour	Summary of Events and Information	Remarks and references to Appendices
	SEPT 1917.		VOL. VI	
VLAMERTINGHE H8. C. 7. 6. SHEET 28.	1st to 13th.		Fatigues on R.A. Ammunition Dumps.	[initials]
	14th.		8 O.R's attached for fatigues at VANCOUVER DUMP. H8. D. 7. 3.	
	19th.		9 O.R's attached 210th Bde. R.F.A.	[initials]
	20th to 29.		Fatigue on VANCOUVER DUMP & with 210th Bde R.F.A.	
	29th.		16 O.R's return from DUMP & 210th Bde.	
	30th.		Proceed by motor lorries to WORMHOUT, en route for COXYDE les Bains	[initials]
	30th.		Arrive WORMHOUT & encamp for the night.	

A Hesketh [signature]
Capt R.F.A.
D.T.M.O.
42 Div Arty

T2134. Wt. W708—776. 500000. 4/15. Sir J. C. & S.

Instructions regarding War Diaries and Intelligence Summaries are contained in F. S. Regs., Part II. and the Staff Manual respectively. Title pages will be prepared in manuscript.

Army Form C. 2118.

WAR DIARY "V42" TRENCH MORTAR BATTERY
or
~~INTELLIGENCE SUMMARY.~~
(Erase heading not required.)

SEPTEMBER. 1917.

Place	Date	Hour	Summary of Events and Information	Remarks and references to Appendices
	SEPT 1917		VOL VI.	
VLAMERTINGHE H8. C.7.6. SHEET 28.	1st to 5th		Fatigues on R.A. Ammunition Dump & usual fatigues in the Line	[initials]
	6th	7AM.	3 Rounds 9.45" Bombs fired by Heavy Trench Mortar on BECK HOUSE. Mortar put out of action after 3rd round. 1 O.R. killed.	[initials]
	7th to 10th		Fatigues on R.A. Ammunition Dumps & in the Line	[initials]
	11th	7.30 PM to 8 PM.	5 Rounds 9.45" Bombs fired by H.T.M. on Strong Point D25. B.1.5.	
	11th		2nd Heavy Mortar taken in the Line – 1 O.R. killed	[initials]
	12th		E.A. dropped bombs in vicinity of camp – 1. O.R. severely wounded (Z Batty).	
	13th		Heavy Gun emplacement destroyed by shell-fire – gun not damaged – 6" Mortar emplacement destroyed by shell-fire & gun damaged.	[initials]
	14th to 15th		Fatigues in Line & R.A. Dumps.	
	17th		1 Heavy Trench Mortar taken out of the Line	[initials]

Continued :–

T2134. Wt. W708–776. 500000. 4/15. Sir J. C. & S.

Instructions regarding War Diaries and Intelligence Summaries are contained in F. S. Regs., Part II. and the Staff Manual respectively. Title pages will be prepared in manuscript.

WAR DIARY V42 HEAVY TRENCH MORTARS.
or
~~INTELLIGENCE SUMMARY.~~
(Erase heading not required.)

Army Form C. 2118.

Place	Date	Hour	Summary of Events and Information	Remarks and references to Appendices
	Sept 1917.		Vol VI Continued.	
VLAMERTINGHE H8.c.7.6. Sheet 28.	18th		Usual fatigues.	
	19th		1 Officer + 20 ORs attached 210th Bde R.F.A.	
			13. O.R's attached 211th Bde R.F.A.	[initials]
	25th		2nd Heavy Trench Mortar brought out of the Line.	
	26th		1. N.C.O. attached 210th Bde. R.F.A.	[initials]
	27th		1 Officer + 1 O.R. attached 210th Bde R.F.A.	
	29th		2 Officers + 15 O.R's returned from 210th Bde R.F.A.	[initials]
	29th	7 PM to midnight	E.A. dropped a large number of bombs on VLAMERTINGHE + vicinity - no damage to T.M. Personnel.	
	30th	9 AM	Proceed by motor lorries to WORMHOUT	
	30th		Arrive WORMHOUT + encamp for the night.	[initials]

[signature]
Capt. R.F.A.
D.T.M.O.
47 Div Arty.

T2134. Wt. W708—776. 500000. 4/15. Sir J. C. & S.

18

Vol 7

CONFIDENTIAL.

WAR DIARY. OF

42ND. DIVN. TRENCH MORTARS. R.A.

FROM. 1ST OCTOBER 1917. TO. 31ST. OCTOBER. 1917.

VOLUMN VII.

Instructions regarding War Diaries and Intelligence Summaries are contained in F. S. Regs., Part II. and the Staff Manual respectively. Title pages will be prepared in manuscript.

WAR DIARY 42 DIVN. R.A. TRENCH MORTAR BRIGADE or ~~INTELLIGENCE SUMMARY.~~ OCTOBER 1917.

Army Form C. 2118.

(Erase heading not required.)

Place	Date	Hour	Summary of Events and Information — Sheet I.	Remarks and references to Appendices
			VOL VII.	
WORMHOUT.	1.10.17		Proceed by motor lorries to TETEGHEM.	HHh
TETEGHEM	2.10.17		Proceed by motor lorries to COXYDE BAINS - Arrive COXYDE BAINS.	HHh
COXYDE BAINS	3.10.17		All Heavy & 6" Trench Mortars taken over from 66th DIVISION.	HHh
W6. C 8 8.				
-	4.10.17		LEFT DIVISIONAL FRONT. Heavy & medium batteries relieve 1st Division TM's in the line & take over all guns & emplacements.	HHh
			NOTE. 42nd & 1st Trench Mortar alternately mann the guns.	HHh
-	5.10.17		5 Round 9.45" Bombs & 25 Round 2" Bombs fired on M14. B.2.3. Several direct hits obtained & much timber & iron blown into the air.	HHh
-	9.10.17		6 rounds 2" bombs fired on enemy T.M. M15. C 2.9. in retaliation to hostile T.M firing.	HHh
-	10.10.17		All batteries relieved by the 1st. Division T.M.B.	HHh
-	12.10.17		All guns & positions taken over by 41st Division T.M.B	HHh
-	13.10.17		Brigade moves to COXYDE - all guns & positions taken over from 32nd Div.	HHh
COXYDE	13.10.17	11AM	RIGHT DIVISIONAL FRONT. Heavy TM's fired 3 rounds on GREY GABLES	
X13. B. 7 8			M18 C.3.1 in retaliation to hostile T.M fire.	HHh
SHEET 11SE.				

CONTINUED.

T2134. Wt. W708—776. 500000. 4/15. Sir J. C. & S.

Instructions regarding War Diaries and Intelligence Summaries are contained in F. S. Regs., Part II. and the Staff Manual respectively. Title pages will be prepared in manuscript.

WAR DIARY
or
~~INTELLIGENCE SUMMARY.~~
(Erase heading not required.)

42 DIVN TRENCH MORTAR BRIGADE RA.

Army Form C. 2118.

Place	Date	Hour	Summary of Events and Information Sheet 2	Remarks and references to Appendices
	OCTOBER. 1917		VOL VII CONTINUED.	
COXYDE X13.B.7.8. SHEET 11.SE	13.10.17	5 P.M.	Heavy T.M's fired 5 rounds, retaliation to hostile T.M. which was active at M17.C 60.25. The second round caused a fire which lasted about 10 minutes. Enemy ceased firing.	HHh
	14.10.17	9 AM	Heavy T.M's fired 4 rounds on hostile TM active at PEONY HOUSE M24 A 55.40. Enemy silenced.	HHh
	–	5.30 P.M.	Heavy T.Ms fired 2 rounds retaliation on hostile T.M. at THE PIPERS M17.C 60.25.	
	15.10.17		1st DIVISION TRENCH MORTARS withdrawn from 42nd Division Command.	HHh
	15.10.17	11.15 A.M.	Heavy TMs fired 3 rounds retaliatory fire on enemy TM at THE PIPERS M17.C 60.25.	HHh
	–	1.30 P.M.	8 rounds were fired by Heavy T.Ms on hostile TM at GREY GABLES M18.C 35.10. The 3rd round caused a small fire & enemy ceased firing.	HHh
	16.10.17	12.30 A.M.	Heavy TMs fired 5 rounds in retaliation to active hostile T.M at PITTE HOUSE M23.A50.75.	HHh
	–	6.30. P.M.	Enemy TM firing from PITTE HOUSE – 3 rounds heavies fired in retaliation & enemy ceased firing.	HHh
			CONTINUED.–	

T2134. Wt. W708—776. 500000. 4/15. Sir J. C. & S.

Instructions regarding War Diaries and Intelligence Summaries are contained in F. S. Regs., Part II. and the Staff Manual respectively. Title pages will be prepared in manuscript.

WAR DIARY
or
~~INTELLIGENCE SUMMARY.~~
(*Erase heading not required.*)

42nd TRENCH MORTAR BRIGADE RA.

Army Form C. 2118.

Place	Date	Hour	Summary of Events and Information Sheet 3.	Remarks and references to Appendices
HEADQUARTERS	OCTOBER	1917.	VOL VII CONTINUED.	
COXYDE	17.10.17	2 PM	10 rounds heavy T.M's fired on hostile TM at MIMOSA M23. b 4 7. causing	[illegible]
X13. B 7 8			3 fires - Two dug-outs are believed to have been penetrated.	
SHEET 11 SE.		3.30 PM.	In retaliation to hostile TM firing, heavy TMs opened fire on	[illegible]
			M23. b 47. During the shoot 2 enemy TMs were observed firing	
			from M17. C. 2. 4. Our Heavy TMs switched on to these & secured a	
			direct hit. Enemy ceased firing. 12 rounds fired in all.	
	18.10.17	6.15 [illegible]	3 rounds heavies fired on GREY GABLES M18. C 3.1	
		6.45 PM	3 rounds on BRACKEN HOUSE M17. D 40. 25 & MINE HOUSE M23 b. 1. 8,	[illegible]
			retaliation to hostile light T M's which were silenced.	
		8 PM [illegible]	Heavy T.Ms fired 3 rounds on OAK HOUSE M23. A 70. 99 & PINE HOUSE. }	[illegible]
		8.30 PM.	3 rounds on BLOCK HOUSE and MINE HOUSE }	
			1 round on MIMOSA HOUSE M23 b. 65. 75 in retaliation. }	
	19.10.17	1.15 AM	6 rounds Heavy T.Ms fired on German Support Line from PINE HOUSE	
			to MINE HOUSE.	[illegible]
		3.30 AM.	5 rounds Heavy T.Ms fired on GREY GABLES & 5 rounds on BLOCK HOUSE	
			and MINE HOUSE in retaliation.	[illegible]
			CONTINUED	

T2134. Wt. W708—776. 500000. 4/15. Sir J. C. & S.

Instructions regarding War Diaries and Intelligence Summaries are contained in F. S. Regs., Part II. and the Staff Manual respectively. Title pages will be prepared in manuscript.

WAR DIARY or ~~INTELLIGENCE SUMMARY.~~

(*Erase heading not required.*)

42 DIV. TRENCH MORTAR BRIGADE R.A.

Army Form C. 2118.

Sheet 4

Place	Date	Hour	Summary of Events and Information	Remarks and references to Appendices
HEADQUARTERS.	OCTOBER 1917.		VOL VII CONTINUED.	
COXYDE.	19th/10/17	4 PM.	Heavy T Ms fired 5 rounds registration on GREY GABLES.	JHH
X13. B 7 8	20.10.17	9.15 AM	Heavy T Ms fired 3 rounds on CROSS ROADS. M23. b. 95. 90.	JHH
SHEET. 11. S.E	21.10.17	2.30 PM.	Heavy T Ms fired 3 rounds registration on PINE HOUSE and LOMBARTZYDE CROSS ROADS.	JHH
		4. PM	Heavies fired 4 rounds retaliation on MINE HOUSE.	
		8 PM	- - 4 - - - PINE HOUSE	
			18 rounds 6" Newton fired on hostile T M M15. D 95. 35. Enemy silenced.	
	22.10.17.		14 - Heavy T.M.s fired on hostile TMs LOMBARDZYDE CROSS ROADS in retaliation	JHH
			15 - - - - - - - at the PIPERS in retaliation.	
	24.10.17.	4.30 PM.	6 rounds fired by Heavy on hostile TMs M17. C 35 40. Enemy ceased firing after 1st round. Our 3rd round caused a small fire.	JHH
	25th.	6.45 AM.	6 rounds Heavy TMs fired on enemy T.M at the GREY GABLES. Enemy silenced after 2nd round.	JHH
		8.30 AM	3 rounds Heavies fired on PINE HOUSE M23. a 50. 80.	JHH
		2.0 PM	4 - - - - PEONY HOUSE M24. a 50. 45 in retaliation to hostile T. Ms.	JHH

CONTINUED

T2134. Wt. W708—776. 500000. 4/15. Sir J. C. & S.

Instructions regarding War Diaries and Intelligence Summaries are contained in F. S. Regs., Part II. and the Staff Manual respectively. Title pages will be prepared in manuscript.

WAR DIARY
or
~~INTELLIGENCE~~ SUMMARY.
(Erase heading not required.)

42 DIV TRENCH MORTAR BRIGADE RA.

OCTOBER 1917.

Army Form C. 2118.

Sheet 5

Place	Date	Hour	Summary of Events and Information	Remarks and references to Appendices
	OCTOBER 1917.		VOL VII	
COXYDE.	26.10.17	2.30 PM	9 rounds 6" NEWTONS fired on M.G. EMPLACEMENT M16. C 14 32.	JHL
X13. B. 7. 8			2 - 6" - fired, registration on H.T.M. EMPLACEMENT M15. D. 96 34.	
SHEET 11 S.E.	27.10.17	7.30 PM	6 - Heavies fired on ROSE HOUSE, retaliation to hostile TM fire	JHL
	28.10.17		7 - 6" NEWTONS fired on hostile HTM M15. d. 96 34 in retaliation - enemy ceased firing.	JHL
		6.45 AM	Hostile T.M. observed firing from PEONY HOUSE M24 a 5 5. 2 Heavy T.M.s fired in retaliation & silenced enemy. 21 rounds fired. Large pieces of timber & concrete were blown up.	JHL
		2.30 PM.	12 rounds H T.M.s fired on enemy T.M. firing from GREY GABLES M18. C 3 1. Enemy ceased firing after 5th round.	JHL
		6.30 PM.	Trench Mortar silenced, which had been active at LILAC HOUSE - 7 Rounds H.T.M.s fired in retaliation.	JHL
	29.10.17	7.30 AM	6 rounds HTMs fired on hostile TM ROSE HOUSE M 24 a. 2 7. Enemy silenced.	
		12 Midnight	10 - - - . the PIPERS M17 C. 69 25. Small fire caused - pitprops & other material blown up. Enemy ceased firing.	JHL

CONTINUED.

T2134. Wt. W708—776. 500000. 4/15. Sir J. C. & S.

Instructions regarding War Diaries and Intelligence Summaries are contained in F. S. Regs., Part II. and the Staff Manual respectively. Title pages will be prepared in manuscript.

WAR DIARY or ~~INTELLIGENCE SUMMARY.~~

(Erase heading not required.)

42nd Div. Trench Mortars. R.A.

October. 1917.

Army Form C. 2118.

Place	Date	Hour	Summary of Events and Information — Sheet 6.	Remarks and references to Appendices
	October. 1917.		Vol VII Continued.	
Coxyde. Headquarters.	30.10.17	11.55 P.M.	Hostile T.M. active at the Pipers. HTMs fired 6 rounds in retaliation & silenced enemy.	[initials]
X13.B.7.8 Sheet 11-SE.	31.10.17	2.10 A.M.	Hostile T.M. again active at the Pipers. 5 rounds HTMs fired in retaliation.	[initials]
		3 AM	3 rounds HTMs fired in retaliation on Peony House.	
			9 - 6" Newtons fired on Mamelon Vert - registration on S.O.S. 3 rounds made direct hits on the trench.	
		9.30 AM.	3 rounds HTMs fired on Grey Gables	[initials]
		3.45 P.M.	15 - 6" Newtons fired on enemy's wire & trench M.19.c.5.4. 6 of the rounds fell into the wire and cut a gap 20' wide. Remainder of bombs distributed on Rope Walk to cover the real intention, ie, to cut wire. Enemy retaliated very promptly with salvoes of 4.2s directly on gun position. 1 OR was slightly wounded & one of the gun-pits had a direct hit, setting camouflage on fire. The enemy today flooded trenches opposite Lombartzyde Sector.	[initials]

[signature]
Capt RFA
D.T.M.O.
42 Div Arty.

T2134. Wt. W708—776. 500000. 4/15. Sir J. C. & S.

CONFIDENTIAL.

WAR DIARY.

of.

42ND. DIVISIONAL. TRENCH MORTAR. BRIGADE. R.A.

FROM NOVEMBER 1st 1917 — TO. NOVEMBER. 30TH 1917.

VOLUMN VIII

Instructions regarding War Diaries and Intelligence Summaries are contained in F. S. Regs., Part II. and the Staff Manual respectively. Title pages will be prepared in manuscript.

WAR DIARY 42nd DIV TRENCH MORTARS R.A.
or
~~INTELLIGENCE SUMMARY.~~
(Erase heading not required.)

Army Form C. 2118.

NOVEMBER 1917.

Place	Date	Hour	Summary of Events and Information	Remarks and references to Appendices
			VOL VIII	
COXYDE	1.11.17.	2. P.M.	4 rounds 9.45" bombs fired on the PIPERS in retaliation, the 4th round caused a small fire & enemy ceased firing.	
X 13. B. 7 8.			9 rounds 6" NEWTON bombs fired on hostile H.T.M. M15. D 96.34 in retaliation	
BELGIUM SHEET 11 S.E: 1: 20000		10.5 P.M.	6 rounds 9.45" bombs fired on T.M. at GREY GABLES, in retaliation at request of Infantry.	[illegible]
	2.11.17.		38 rounds 9.45" bombs fired, neutralization of hostile T.Ms at THE PIPERS, MINE HOUSE, PEONY HOUSE, MINOSA and GREY GABLES. Enemy silenced.	[illegible]
	3rd 11.17	10.15 A.M.	5 rounds 9.45 bombs fired on the PIPERS - direct hits obtained and 3 fires caused.	[illegible]
			5 rounds 9.45" bombs fired on PEONY HOUSE	
		12.45 P.M.	5 rounds 9.45" bombs fired on active hostile T.M. M 23. a 95.85 in cooperation with Heavy Artillery. One direct hit obtained	
			1 round 9.45" fired on T.M. Nr LOMBARTZYDE CHURCH.	
		3.15 P.M.	In retaliation to hostile T.M firing - 5 rounds 9.45" were fired on THE PIPERS - Direct hit obtained & enemy ceased firing	
		5 P.M.	5 rounds 9.45" bombs fired on the PIPERS } In neutralization of hostile T.Ms	
		9.15 -	6 " " " " LILAC & PEONY HOUSE }	

CONTINUED

T2134. Wt. W708—776. 500000. 4/15. Sir J. C. & S.

Instructions regarding War Diaries and Intelligence Summaries are contained in F. S. Regs., Part II. and the Staff Manual respectively. Title pages will be prepared in manuscript.

WAR DIARY or ~~INTELLIGENCE SUMMARY.~~ 42/ Div Trench Mortars RA.

(*Erase heading not required.*)

Army Form C. 2118.

Place	Date	Hour	Summary of Events and Information	Remarks and references to Appendices
	NOVEMBER 1917.		VOL VIII CONTINUED.	
COXYDE	4.11.17	1. AM.	3 rounds 9.45" bombs fired on hostile T.M. Nr LOMBARTZYDE CHURCH.	
X13 b. 7 8		1.30 AM	2 - - - - - - - - at THE PIPERS.	
SHEET 11 SE 1/20000		6.0 -	3 - - - - - - - - THE PIPERS.	
			3 - - - - - - - - Nr LOMBARTZYDE CHURCH.	
		10.30 PM.	5 - - - - - - - - Nr LOMBARTZYDE CHURCH	
	6.11.17	2.20 AM.	6 - - - - - - - - at PEONY HOUSE and LILAC HOUSE.	
		6. AM	8 - - - - - - - - Nr LOMBARTZYDE CHURCH	
		7.30 -	6 - - - - - - - - at LILAC HOUSE	
		3.30 PM	7 - - - - - - - - at GREY GABLES.	
	6.11.17	4 AM	6 - - - - - BAMBURGH TRENCH.	
		6 AM	14 - - - - - hostile TMs Nr LOMBARTZYDE CHURCH and PIPERS A direct hit was obtained & 2 large fires caused. Enemy ceased firing	
		8.45 AM	6 rounds 9.45 bombs fired on hostile TMs at LILAC HOUSE	
			8 - - - - - - - - Nr LOMBARTZYDE CHURCH and at M17 D 0.2 and M17. C 6 3. Large fires caused enemy silenced	
		11.30 AM	11 rounds 9.45" bombs fired on same targets	
		2.30 PM	9 - - - - - - THE PIPERS	
			CONTINUED	

T2134. Wt. W708—776. 500000. 4/15. Sir J. C. & S.

Instructions regarding War Diaries and Intelligence Summaries are contained in F. S. Regs., Part II. and the Staff Manual respectively. Title pages will be prepared in manuscript.

WAR DIARY or ~~INTELLIGENCE~~ SUMMARY.

42 Div TRENCH MORTARS RA.

(Erase heading not required.)

Army Form C.2118.

Place	Date	Hour	Summary of Events and Information	Remarks and references to Appendices
			VOL VIII CONTINUED	
COXYDE	7.11.17	6.30AM.	5 rounds 9.45" bombs fired on active hostile T.M. M17.C 15.15 in retaliation	[initials]
X13.b.78		7.30	1 - - - - - - TM. Nr LOMBARTZYDE CHURCH.	
SHEET 11 SE			4 - - - - - - - M17 C.O.4. a direct hit obtained & enemy silenced	
1.20000.			2 - 6" NEWTONS fired - registration on S.O.S.	
		5.15 PM	8 - 9.45" bombs fired on T.M.s Nr LOMBARTZYDE CHURCH	
		12 midnight	2 - - - - - - - - -	
	8.11.17	8.15AM.	8 - - - - - - - at the PIPERS in neutralization	[initials]
		9.45AM	2 - - - - - - Nr LOMBARTZYDE CHURCH do.	
		4.30 PM.	4 - - - - - - at the PIPERS. do.	
		5.0	1 - - - - - - NEAR LOMBARTZYDE CHURCH do	[initials]
	9.11.17	9.15 AM	3 - - - - - - at the PIPERS do	
		3.45 PM	5 - - - - - - M16. D. 80.35 do	
		4.20 PM	4 - - - - - - M17. C 3.3. do	
		8.30	3 - - - - - - at THE PIPERS do.	
	10.11.17	8.15 AM	3 - - - - - - at THE PIPERS do	[initials]
		3.45 PM	5 - - - - - - M23 a 95 90 causing small fire do	
		4.30 PM	4 - - - - - - at THE PIPERS do.	

T2134. Wt. W708—776. 500000. 4/15. Sir J. C. & S.

Instructions regarding War Diaries and Intelligence Summaries are contained in F. S. Regs., Part II. and the Staff Manual respectively. Title pages will be prepared in manuscript.

WAR DIARY
or
INTELLIGENCE SUMMARY.

(Erase heading not required.)

42/Div Trench Mortars R.A.

Army Form C. 2118.

Place	Date	Hour	Summary of Events and Information	Remarks and references to Appendices
			VOL VIII CONTINUED.	
	NOVR			
COXYDE	11.11.17	9.30AM.	4 rounds 9.45" bombs fired on the PIPERS - in neutralization of hostile T.M's -	
X13. b 7.8		3.15 PM	4 - - - - - T.M. M17 c 95. 20. do do	[initials]
SHEET 11 S.E.		6.45 -	11 - - - - - at THE PIPERS do do.	
1:20000.	12.11.17	2 PM	6 - NEWTON 6" - - - M15. D. 95.35 do do	
		3.15	8 - - 9.45" bombs - - - at THE PIPERS do do	[initials]
	14.11.17	9.15AM	4 - - - - - - - THE PIPERS do do	
		2.45 PM	6 - - - - - - - THE PIPERS do do	[initials]
		4.45 -	1 - - - - - - - THE PIPERS do do	
		11.30 PM	4 - - - - - - - OAK HOUSE do do	
	15.11.17	8.30 AM.	3 - - - - - - - THE PIPERS do do	
		9.15 -	3 - - - - - - NEAR LOMBARTZYDE CHURCH. do do	[initials]
		3.30 PM	8 - - - - - - NEAR LOMBARTZYDE CHURCH. do do	
		4.0 -	3 - - - - - - at THE PIPERS do do	
		10.30 -	2 - - - - - - NEAR LOMBARTZYDE CHURCH. do do	
	16.11.17	2.20AM	3 - - - - - - NEAR LOMBARTZYDE CHURCH do do.	
		2.0 PM	10 - 6" NEWTONS - - T.M. M15. D. 96. 34 do do	[initials]
		3.0 -	8 - 9.45 Bombs - - TM NEAR LOMBARTZYDE CHURCH & PIPERS CONTINUED.	

T2134. Wt. W708-776. 500000. 4/15. Sir J. C. & S.

Instructions regarding War Diaries and Intelligence Summaries are contained in F. S. Regs., Part II. and the Staff Manual respectively. Title pages will be prepared in manuscript.

WAR DIARY or ~~INTELLIGENCE SUMMARY.~~ 42 DIV TRENCH MORTARS RA

(Erase heading not required.)

Army Form C. 2118.

Place	Date	Hour	Summary of Events and Information	Remarks and references to Appendices
			VOL VIII CONTINUED	
COXYDE	NOUR	1 AM	4 rounds fired by Heavy Trench Mortars on T.M. NEAR LOMBARTZYDE CHURCH	
X13.b.78	17th 1917	12.30 PM	2 - - - - - - - - NEAR LOMBARTZYDE CHURCH	JMh
	18.11.17	12.45 PM	3 - - - - - - - - M17 C 15 15.	
		4.0 PM	5 - - - - - - - - M17 C 15 15	
			12 - NEWTON 6" fired on hostile T.M's M15. D 96. 34	JMh
		9.15 PM	2 - 9.45" bombs - - - - at THE PIPERS.	
			3 - NEWTON 6" - - - - at M15 D 96 34	
	19.11.17	2.45 AM	2 - 9.45" bombs - - - - at THE PIPERS	
	19.11.17		16 - - - - - - - - THE PIPERS + LOMBARTZYDE CHURCH	JMh
			In neutralization of hostile Trench Mortars	
	19.11.17		All Heavy & Medium Batteries withdrawn from the line, having been relieved by the 133rd FRENCH DIVISION	
	19.11.17		9 NEWTON MORTARS 6" and 2 ENGLISH TRENCH MORTARS 9.45" LONG withdrawn from the line	
	20.11.17		All Trench Mortars handed over to the XV CORPS	JMh
	22.11.17	8.0 AM	Brigade proceeds by motor lorries to FONTES - arrive 7.0 PM. 22/11/17.	
FONTES	30.11.17	8.0	Brigade proceeds by Motor lorries to CALONNE-SUR-LA LYS.	JMh

T2134. Wt. W708—776. 500000. 4/15. Sir J. C. & S.

Instructions regarding War Diaries and Intelligence Summaries are contained in F. S. Regs., Part II. and the Staff Manual respectively. Title pages will be prepared in manuscript.

WAR DIARY
or
~~INTELLIGENCE SUMMARY.~~

(Erase heading not required.)

42nd Div Trench Mortar Brigade R.A.

Army Form C. 2118.

Place	Date	Hour	Summary of Events and Information	Remarks and references to Appendices
			VOL VIII CONTINUED.	
CALONNE SUR-LA-LYS. FRANCE SHEET 36A.	30/1/1917.	10 AM.	Brigade proceeds by Motor lorries to BEUVRY and relieves the 25th DIVISION in the line.	[illegible]

[illegible signature]
Capt R.F.A.
DTMO
42 Division

T2134. Wt. W708—776. 500000. 4/15. Sir J. C. & S.

Vol 9

CONFIDENTIAL

WAR DIARY

of

42nd TRENCH MORTAR BRIGADE R.A.

FROM 1st DECEMBER 1917. TO 31st DECEMBER 1917.

VOL. IX.

D.T.M.O.,
42nd DIVISION.
No. 18/52
Date 31.12.1917

To
The Staff Captain R.A.
R.A. Headquarters 42/Div

Enclosed please find War Diary for 42nd Trench Mortar Brigade R.A. for Month of December 1917.

[signature]

Capt R.F.A.
D.T.M.O.
42/Div Arty.

Army Form C. 2118.

Instructions regarding War Diaries and Intelligence Summaries are contained in F. S. Regs., Part II. and the Staff Manual respectively. Title pages will be prepared in manuscript.

WAR DIARY
or
~~INTELLIGENCE SUMMARY.~~
(Erase heading not required.)

42nd TRENCH MORTARS. R.A.

DECEMBER 1917.

Place	Date	Hour	Summary of Events and Information	Remarks and references to Appendices
			VOL IX.	
	Decr 1917.			
BEUVRY. F20.a.8.9	3rd	8 AM	5 rounds 2" bombs fired on FRANKS KEEP in retaliation to hostile T.M. fire.	[initials]
BETHUNE	4th	7.30 AM.	5 rounds 2" bombs fired on enemy T.M. BRICKSTACKS in retaliation.	[initials]
Combined sheet 36A SE 36 S.W.	5th	10.30 AM to 12 noon.	17 " 2" " " registration on S.O.S. Lines.	[initials]
36A NE 36B NW		2.0 PM	15 " 2" " " " " " "	[initials]
FRANCE 1:40000.			4 " 2" " " on A9. d. 9 3½.	[initials]
		2.30 PM	7 " 9.45" " " on BRICKSTACKS.	[initials]
	6th	3.0 PM	2 " 9.45" " " registration on CROSS ROADS. A10 a 7.8.	
			4 " 9.45" " " on JERUSALEM HILL.	
		3.15 PM	11 " 2" " " on granatenwerfer A9. B.2.3 in retaliation.	
			15 " 2" " " on A9. B. 8 0 in retaliation	
			15 " 2" " " " A10.C. 10.25. "	[initials]
		3-3.15 PM	10 " 2" " " " FRANKS KEEP. "	
			10 " 2" " " " A22 a 2 4 "	
			10 " 2" " " " A16. D. 5 0 "	

CONTINUED :-

T2134. Wt. W708—776. 500000. 4/15. Sir J. C. & S.

Army Form C. 2118.

Instructions regarding War Diaries and Intelligence Summaries are contained in F. S. Regs., Part II. and the Staff Manual respectively. Title pages will be prepared in manuscript.

WAR DIARY
or
~~INTELLIGENCE~~ SUMMARY.
(Erase heading not required.)

42nd DIV R.A. TRENCH MORTARS.

DECEMBER 1917

Place	Date	Hour	Summary of Events and Information	Remarks and references to Appendices
	DECR 1917		VOL IX Continued.	
BEUVRY	7th	11.30AM.	5 round 2" bombs fired on FRANKS KEEP in retaliation to hostile HTM fire.	[initials]
F20.a 8 9	8th	3.30PM	10 - 2" " " " JERUSALEM HILL A22 a 55 90 in retaliation	[initials]
			15 - 2" " " " SUNKEN ROAD TRENCH A9 b. 30.45 in -	
	9th	9.20AM	1 - 9.45" " " " TM A22 a. 95 75 in retaliation	
		3.PM	10 - 2" " " " TM. A22 a 15 10 - -	
			15 - 2" " " " A9 d 95 60 - -	[initials]
			11 - 2" " " " A10 c. 15 60 - -	
			7 - 2" " " " A9. b. 35 45 - -	
		3.30PM	16 - 2" " " " A22 a 50.85 - -	
		5.0 -	2 - 9.45" " " " A22 c 5 4 - -	
	10th	8.30AM.	6 - 2" " " " A22 a 1 6 - -	
		2.0PM	8 - 6" " " " A10 a 9 8 - -	
		12.15 -	1 - 9.45" " " " A4 d 15 65 Registration	
		3.0 -	9 - 9.45" " " " A4 d 15 65 & A4 c 60.45.	[initials]
			6 - 2" " " " A22 a 5 8	
			20 - 2" " " " A22 c 2 9	

CONTINUED.

T2134. Wt. W708—776. 500000. 4/15. Sir J. C. & S.

Instructions regarding War Diaries and Intelligence Summaries are contained in F. S. Regs., Part II. and the Staff Manual respectively. Title pages will be prepared in manuscript.

WAR DIARY
or
~~INTELLIGENCE SUMMARY.~~
(Erase heading not required.)

42nd Div TRENCH MORTARS. RA.

CONTINUED

Army Form C. 2118.

Place	Date	Hour	Summary of Events and Information	Remarks and references to Appendices
			VOL IX.	
	DECR. 1917.			
BEUVRY	10th	3.0 PM	20 rounds 6" bombs fired on TM. A10. A10 35 in retaliation	[illegible]
F20 a 8 9.			20 - 6" " " " " A10 A15 70 - -	
			12 - 6" " " " " A10 A 00 55 -	
		3.15 PM.	9 . 2" " " " " A22. A1. 6 - -	
	11th	11.0 AM	5 " 2" " " " " A22 A5 8 - -	[illegible]
		2.15 PM	50 " 6" " " " SAXON WAY, PRUSSIAN WAY and AUSTRIAN WAY.	
		3.0 -	10 " 2" " " " TM. A22 a 4 2. In retaliation	
			4 " 9.45" " " " " A4 c. 9. 8 and A9 d 15 60. Retaliation	
		3.30 -	9 " 2" " " " " A22 a 5 8 "	
		4.0 PM	4 " 2" " " " REDOUBT A15 d. 8. 4 "	
	12th	10.0 AM	10 " 2" " " " TRENCH A9 d 95 87 "	[illegible]
			5 " 2" " " " " A10. c 25 25. "	
		6.30 AM	26 " 2" " " " TM. A22 a 15 80 "	
		4.15 PM.	8 " 2" " " " REDOUBT A15 d. 8. 4 "	
	13th	9 AM - 2 PM	8 " 9.45" " " " group of TMs A22a. A16a & M.G. A16a	[illegible]
		11 AM	2 " 9.45" " " " TM A22 a 95. 80.	

CONTINUED.

T2134. Wt. W708-776. 500000. 4/15. Sir J. C. & S.

Instructions regarding War Diaries and Intelligence Summaries are contained in F. S. Regs., Part II. and the Staff Manual respectively. Title pages will be prepared in manuscript.

WAR DIARY or ~~INTELLIGENCE SUMMARY.~~

(Erase heading not required.)

42nd Div. Trench Mortar Brigade R.A.

Army Form C. 2118.

Place	Date	Hour	Summary of Events and Information	Remarks and references to Appendices
			Vol IX Continued.	
Beuvry	13/12/17	3.0 PM.	5 rounds 2" Bombs fired on TM. a 22. a. 5 2.	
Headquarters.		3-4 PM	33 " 6" " " Communication Trench A10. c 75 05.	
F20. a. 8 9.			33 " 6" " " " " A10 c 75 70	
Bethune			26 " 6" " " " " A10 c 35. 55.	
Combined Sheet	14th.	10.30 AM	15 " 6" " " " T.M. A22. a. 5 2 Retaliation	
36A SE 36 SW		2.0 PM	5 " 2" " " T.M A22 a. 5 2 "	
36c NE 36c NW		3.30	5 " 2" " " " A22 a 5 8 "	
			3 " 9.45" " " " A16 c 9. 7. "	
	15th	12.30 PM	10 " 9.45" " " " A4 A 45 80 "	
		1.30	6 " 9.45 " " " A16. c 8 5 "	
			5 " 2" " " " A22. a. 5 8 "	
		2.30	5 " 2" " " " A22 a 5 8 "	
		2.45	6 " 9.45" " " " A16 c 80 65 "	
		4.0 PM	10 " 2" " " " A22 a 5 8 "	
	16th.	12.30 PM	19 " 6" " " Wire A3. d 5 5.	
			2 " 2" " Tortoise A16 c 80. 65.	
			Continued.	

T2134. Wt. W708—776. 500000. 4/15. Sir J. C. & S.

Instructions regarding War Diaries and Intelligence Summaries are contained in F. S. Regs., Part II. and the Staff Manual respectively. Title pages will be prepared in manuscript.

WAR DIARY
or
~~INTELLIGENCE SUMMARY.~~
(Erase heading not required.)

42nd DIV TRENCH MORTAR BRIGADE R.A.

Army Form C. 2118.

Place	Date	Hour	Summary of Events and Information	Remarks and references to Appendices
	DECEMBER 1917.			
BELLVRY	17th	9 AM	10 round 2" bombs fired on TM. A22 a 5 4. in retaliation	[initials]
F20.a 8 9		11.30	15 " 2" " " " A22 a 5 8 –	
		2 30 PM	16 " 2" " " " Wire TORTOISE A16. d. 55 70.	
		3.0	15 " 2" " " " TM. A22 a 8 8 in retaliation	
			4 " 6" " " " wire A3. d. 55 40.	
	18th	12 15 PM.	5 " 6" " " registration on Group of TM's A22 a 8.6. & A22 a 9 5.	[initials]
	19th	11 am	5 " 2" " " on TM A22 a 8 9 in retaliation	
		3.0 PM	6 " 6" " " " A3. d 9 6	[initials]
			20 " 2" " " " SAXON WAY.	
	20th	2.40 PM	20 " 2" " " " TRENCH JUNCTIONS A9. d 9.9 & A10. c 1 9.	
		11. am	12 " 2" " " " BRICKSTACKS in retaliation	[initials]
			12 " 6" " " " FRANKS KEEP –	
	21st	8.0 AM.	5 " 2" " " " FRANKS KEEP –	
		11.30	20 " 2" " " " A22. c 7.8 and A22 c. 8 4 in retaliation	[initials]
		12 noon	15 " 2" " " " TM A16. c. 50. 45 –	
			16 " 2" " " " TRENCH JUNCTIONS A9. d 95.60. A9 d 95 90. Destructive	shoot
			Continued.	

Instructions regarding War Diaries and Intelligence Summaries are contained in F. S. Regs., Part II. and the Staff Manual respectively. Title pages will be prepared in manuscript.

WAR DIARY
or
~~INTELLIGENCE SUMMARY.~~
(Erase heading not required.)

T 42nd DIV. TRENCH MORTARS RA.

Army Form C. 2118.

Place	Date	Hour	Summary of Events and Information	Remarks and references to Appendices
	DECEMBER 1917.		VOL IX CONTINUED.	
BEUVRY	21st	12.10 PM.	10 rounds 6" bombs fired on TM. A4 c 50 15 and A4 c 15 05. } in retaliation	[initials]
F20. a 8 9			10 " 6" " " " A10. d 20 70 } Destructive & retaliatory	
Bethune }		1.30 PM.	8 " 9.45" " " " TM A4 a 45 75 in retaliation	
Combined sheet }		1.45	6 " 9.45" " " " " A4. d 2 6 "	
France 1:40000		3.30	20 " 6" " " Registration on A22 c.	
	22nd	3.0 PM	4 " 6" " " on D and E BRICKSTACKS	[initials]
		3.30	8 " 6" " " registration on FRANKS KEEP	
	23rd	9 AM	10 " 6" " " on BRICKSTACKS in retaliation	[initials]
		11.30	10 " 6" " " " " "	
		12 noon	28 " 6" " " " TM A4. c 45 15 "	
			15 " 6" " " " " A10 c 10 85	
			7 " 2" " " TRENCH JUNCTIONS A9 d 99 60 and A9 d 95 90 - Destructive shoot.	
			15 " 2" " " " TM A10 c 20 55. in retaliation	
		12.20 PM	11 " 9.45" " " " A4 c. 45 15 " "	
		3.30	16 " 6" " " " SUPPORT LINE from A22 c 3.9 to A22. c 2 1. }	
			Destructive fire. Several direct hits on trench. }	
			CONTINUED.	

T2134. Wt. W708—776. 500000. 4/15. Sir J. C. & S.

Instructions regarding War Diaries and Intelligence Summaries are contained in F. S. Regs., Part II. and the Staff Manual respectively. Title pages will be prepared in manuscript.

WAR DIARY
or
~~INTELLIGENCE SUMMARY.~~
(Erase heading not required.)

42nd TRENCH MORTARS R.A.

Army Form C. 2118.

Place	Date	Hour	Summary of Events and Information	Remarks and references to Appendices
	DECEMBER 1917		VOL IX CONTINUED.	
BEUVRY	24th	8.50AM	10 rounds 6" bombs fired on T.M A4 c. 65 30	JHH
F20. a. 8-9			10 - 6" " " " CAP. CALL. CAM*	
BETHUNE			5 " 2" " " EMBANKMENT REDOUBT.	
Combined Sheet			6 " 9.45" " " A4 c 65 30. & A22 B 15. 70.	
FRANCE 1:40.000		11.15AM	10 " 6" " " " A3. d 8 0	
			7 " 2" " " A10 c 2 5	
			20 6" CAP. CALL CAM. CAPE.	
			5 " 2" " " EMBANKMENT REDOUBT.	
			6 " 9.45" " " " " & A22. a 85 55.	
			Harassing & destructive fire in accordance with 42nd Divisional Artillery Order No 60. Several direct hits were observed on wire and trenches. Timber and boards were scattered by the bursts.	
	"	7.30PM	10 rounds 2" bombs fired on EMBANKMENT REDOUBT & TRENCH JUNCTION A16. c. 9-3.	JHH
			8 - 6" " " CAP. CALL CAM TMs.	
			7 " 6" " " TORTOISE. DOG. DAM. DALE	
			15 " 6" " " FADE	
			4 " 2" " " SAXON WAY.	
			3 " 9.45" " " CAP CALL CAM.	

Continued.

T2134. Wt. W708—776. 500000. 4/15. Sir J. C. & S.

Instructions regarding War Diaries and Intelligence Summaries are contained in F. S. Regs., Part II. and the Staff Manual respectively. Title pages will be prepared in manuscript.

Army Form C. 2118.

WAR DIARY 42nd DIV TRENCH MORTARS RA.
or
~~INTELLIGENCE SUMMARY.~~
(*Erase heading not required.*)

CONTINUED

Place	Date	Hour	Summary of Events and Information	Remarks and references to Appendices
	DECEMBER 1917.		VOL IX	
BEUVRY	24th	9.10 to 9.15 PM.	10 rounds 2" on EMBANKMENT REDOUBT and TRENCH JUNCTION A16. c. 9 3	JHL
F20 a. 8 9			8 - 6" - TMs CAP. CALL. CAM.	
BETHUNE			4 - 6" - TORTOISE & TMs. DOG DAM DALE	
Combined Sheet			15 " 6" on T.M. FADE.	
FRANCE 1' 40.000			5 " 2" on SAXON WAY.	
			3 " 9.45" on TMs CAP CALL CAM.	
		11.40-11.45 PM	5 " 2" on EMBANKMENT REDOUBT.	
			5 " 6" on CAP CALL CAM	
			3 " 9.45" on " " "	
			6 " 6" on TORTOISE and TM's DOG. DAM. DALE	
			15 " 6" on TM FADE.	
			7 " 2" on SAXON WAY.	
			in cooperation with Artillery in a combined Gas & Artillery bombardment. In accordance with 42nd Divisional Artillery order No 59.	
	26th	4 PM	5 rounds 2" on TM. A16. c. 8 0. Enemy TM Activity - quiet.	JHL
			CONTINUED.	

T2134. Wt. W708—776. 500000. 4/15. Sir J. C. & S.

Army Form C. 2118.

Instructions regarding War Diaries and Intelligence Summaries are contained in F. S. Regs., Part II. and the Staff Manual respectively. Title pages will be prepared in manuscript.

WAR DIARY or ~~INTELLIGENCE SUMMARY.~~ 42nd Div TRENCH MORTARS RA.

(Erase heading not required.)

Place	Date	Hour	Summary of Events and Information	Remarks and references to Appendices
	DECEMBER 1917.		VOL IX CONTINUED.	
BEUVRY	27th	11.30AM.	5 rounds 2" on TM A16. C. 8. 0 in retaliation	JHh
F20 a. 8. 9		2.15PM	10 " 2" " RAILWAY EMBANKMENT and TM A16. C. 8. 0 in retaliation	
BETHUNE Combined			10 " 2" " TM. A22. a 4. 7.	
Sheet. France		2.30-3.0PM.	10 " 2" " TRENCH A9. d 90. 85 } Destruction shoot. Several	
1: 40000.			5 " 2" " " A9. d 97. 62 } direct hits obtained on enemy's	
			7 " 2" " A10 C 25 55 } Wire & trenches. Much timber	
			8 " 2" " A10 C 00. 95 } & debris thrown up & trenches	
			10 " 6" " TORTOISE A16. C 57 } greatly damaged.	
	28th	1.30PM.	7 " 2" " TRENCH A9 d 90 85 } direct hits on trenches.	JHh
			8. " 2" " A9 d 95 60. }	
	29th	2.0PM.	5 " 2" " RAILWAY EMBANKMENT. }	
		2.45	7 " 6" " TM. A16. C 8. 0. } In retaliation. enemy silenced	
		3.0	20 " 6" " CAP. CALL CAM. }	
		3.45	4 " 9.45" " TORTOISE }	JHh
	30th	11.30AM.	15 " 6" " FRANKS KEEP in retaliation - enemy silenced	JHh
		12 noon	18 " 6" " FADE.	
			CONTINUED.	

T2134. Wt. W708—776. 500000. 4/15. Sir J. C. & S.

Instructions regarding War Diaries and Intelligence Summaries are contained in F. S. Regs., Part II. and the Staff Manual respectively. Title pages will be prepared in manuscript.

WAR DIARY 42nd Div Trench Mortars R.A. or ~~INTELLIGENCE SUMMARY.~~

(Erase heading not required.)

Army Form C. 2118.

Place	Date	Hour	Summary of Events and Information	Remarks and references to Appendices
	December 1917.		Vol IX Continued.	
Beuvry	30th	2.30 PM.	20 rounds 6" on Brick Bat Alley in retaliation	[initials]
F20.a.8.9.			9 - 9.45" on Pop and Pad TMs. - - enemy silenced.	
Bethune		3.0 -	5 - 6" on Tortoise - -	
Combined sheet		3.35 -	20 - 6" on Sunken Road } Destructive shoot. Good	
France 1: 40000.			20 - 6" on Trench A10 c. 62.70 } results obtained.	
	31st	2.0 PM.	5 - 2" on Embankment Redoubt }	[initials]
			5 - 2" on A22. a. 5. 7. } Destructive and retaliatory.	
		3.0 PM	10 - 6" on Trench Junction A22. c. 3. 5. }	
			10 - 6" on T.Ms. Cad & Cam }	
		11. AM	25 - 6" on Network of Trenches A9. b. 8. 5 }	[initials]
			25 - 6" - - A10 c. 1. 9. } Destructive shoot.	
			15 - 2" on Prussian Way A9. d. 95. 95 }	

[signature]
Capt RFA
DTMO
42/Div Arty

T2134. Wt. W708—776. 500000. 4/15. Sir J. C. & S.

CONFIDENTIAL.

Vol 11

WAR. DIARY.

OF.

42ND DIVISION TRENCH MORTAR BRIGADE. R.A.

FROM 1ST JANUARY. 1918.

TO. 31ST JANUARY. 1918.

VOLUME X.

Instructions regarding War Diaries and Intelligence Summaries are contained in F. S. Regs., Part II. and the Staff Manual respectively. Title pages will be prepared in manuscript.

WAR DIARY or ~~INTELLIGENCE SUMMARY~~. 42ND TRENCH MORTARS. R.A.

(Erase heading not required.)

JANUARY 1918.

Army Form C. 2118.

Place	Date	Hour	Summary of Events and Information	Remarks and references to Appendices
			VOL. X.	
	JANUARY		1918.	
LE PREOL	1st	11.am	50 rounds 6" bombs fired on TRENCH A9. b 8.5 and A10 c 1.9 } Destructive Shoot.	All
Headquarters		11.30.	15 " 2" " " ". PRUSSIAN WAY. }	Co-ordinates
F10 b 5.2.		11.45 AM	5 " 6" " " " TM. CAM. in retaliation	LA BASSEE
Bethune		12.30 PM	20 " 6" " " " SUNKEN ROAD TRENCH A9 b 72.52 Destructive shoot.	MAP 1:10000 36c N.W.1. Edition 10.A
Combined			5 " 2" " " EMBANKMENT REDOUBT. in retaliation to hostile TM fire.	
Sheet			7 " 9.45" " " " TMs. DAY, DAM and TM at A16. c.90 48 in retaliation	
{36a SE. 36 SW		2.30 b	10 " 2" " " " TRENCH A22 a 5.7.	
(36c NE 36c NW		3.30 Pm	10 " 6" " " " " A27 d 9.5	
1:40000.			15 " 6" " "on TMs CAPE and CART } Destructive & retaliatory.	[illegible]
			10 " 2" " " PRUSSIAN WAY.	
	2nd	10 am	10 " 6" " " " hostile TM FADE. In retaliation enemy silenced	
		11.15.	20 " 6" " " " " " DEAR. DUCK and DEEP in retaliation, }	
			on hostile T.Ms suspected of firing gas bombs.	
		11.30 b	20 bombs 2" fired on TRENCHES A16 c 4 4. A22 a 5 7. In retaliation for T.M. fire	[illegible]
		12.30 PM.	10 - 6" " " " — A22 b 3.6 - - -	
			5 - 6" " " hostile TM CAD in retaliation. Hostile T.M ceased firing	

CONTINUED -

Army Form C. 2118.

Instructions regarding War Diaries and Intelligence Summaries are contained in F. S. Regs., Part II. and the Staff Manual respectively. Title pages will be prepared in manuscript.

WAR DIARY
or
~~INTELLIGENCE SUMMARY.~~
(Erase heading not required.)

42ND DIV TRENCH MORTARS. RA

Place	Date	Hour	Summary of Events and Information	Remarks and references to Appendices
	JANUARY. 1918.		VOL. X. CONTINUED.	
LE PREOL.	2nd.	1.30PM	10 rounds 6" bombs fired on hostile T.Ms. CAPE & CART in retaliation	
–		3.PM	10 " 6" " " " BRICKBAT ALLEY – –	
–		4.45PM	30 " 6" " " " TRENCH A10.A.3.2 in retaliation for T.M. Fire	
–			10 " 2" " " " A9 d 7.7 – – – – –	
–		6.15	6 " 9.45" " " " hostile TMs CAP. CAM. CALL in retaliation. Enemy silenced	[initials]
–	3rd	9.45AM	3 " 9.45" " " " " CAP. CAM CALL – –	[initials]
–	4th.	11.30AM.	22 " 6" " " " TRENCHES A22 c 55 60. A22c 85 90. A22c45.40. A22 c 7.7. Registration by aeroplane – several direct hits reported on trenches.	[initials]
	5th.	8.30AM	20 rounds 6" bombs fired in retaliation on hostile TMs CAM CALL CAPE & CART: Enemy silenced.	
		2.0PM.	22 rounds 6" bombs fired on Mill ABBEY Communication TRENCH in retaliation.	[initials]
	6th.	12 noon	2 " 6" " registration on A3. d. 8.5.	[initials]
		3.30 to 5.30	Hostile T.Ms unusually active, our T.Ms neutralized as follows, in cooperation with Heavy & Field Artillery.	
		3.30 to 5.30PM	6 rounds 9.45" bombs on TM FADE. 27 " 9.45" " " TMs CAP. CAM CALL & A16 c 85.40. A22 b 72.52.	[initials]
			CONTINUED.	

T2134. Wt. W708—776. 500000. 4/15. Sir J. C. & S.

Instructions regarding War Diaries and Intelligence Summaries are contained in F. S. Regs., Part II. and the Staff Manual respectively. Title pages will be prepared in manuscript.

WAR DIARY or ~~INTELLIGENCE SUMMARY.~~

(Erase heading not required.)

42nd DIV TRENCH MORTARS RA.

Army Form C. 2118.

Place	Date	Hour	Summary of Events and Information	Remarks and references to Appendices
	JANUARY 1918.		VOL X CONTINUED.	
LE PREOL.	6th	3.30 to 5.30 PM.	19 rounds 6" bombs on T.M. FADE. 21 " 2" on SUNKEN ROAD TRENCH and S.O.S. Line. 50 " 6" on T.MS. CAP CAM. CALL. CAB CART & CAPE. } In neutralization of hostile T.M fire.	[signature]
	7th	5.20 to 6.35 am.	Enemy T.Ms active on our lines. Our TMs & artillery opened in retaliation and silenced enemy.	[signature]
		5.25 am to 6.35 am.	15 rounds 9.45" bombs on hostile TMs A16 C 85 40. A22 b 72. 52.	
			20 - 6" " on - - CAP. CAM. CALL.	
		10.30 to 12 noon.	18 - 6" " " " CAP CAM. CALL & A16 C 80. 20 in retaliation.	
		1.30 PM.	2 " 2" " " TRENCH. A9 d 97. 29.	
		2.40 to 3.0 PM	7 2" " " " A10 C 5 8.	
		3.55 PM	10 " 6" " " TM. A10 C 18 & trench A10 c 2.6. in retaliation	
		2.30 to 3.30	12 " 9.45" " registration on suspected TMs A16 A 85. 70 A16 C 85 40 A16 A 80 75 A16 a 85 40. A10 a 05 55.	
		4.30 PM.	6 rounds 6" bombs fired on hostile T.M. A16 C 85 25 in retaliation - enemy immediately ceased firing.	[signature]

CONTINUED.

(A7092). Wt. W12839/M1293. 75,0.0. 1/17. D. D. & L., Ltd. Forms/C.2118/14.

Instructions regarding War Diaries and Intelligence Summaries are contained in F. S. Regs., Part II. and the Staff Manual respectively. Title pages will be prepared in manuscript.

WAR DIARY or ~~INTELLIGENCE SUMMARY.~~

(Erase heading not required.)

42ND DIV. TRENCH MORTARS. RA. Army Form C. 2118.

VOL. X. CONTINUED.

Place	Date	Hour	Summary of Events and Information	Remarks and references to Appendices
LE PREOL.	JANUARY 1918.			
	8th	12 noon.	10 rounds 2" bombs fired on M.G. A10c 10.56 in retaliation	
		12.30 PM	18 " 9.45" " " " RAILWAY EMBANKMENT.	
		2.30 -	2 " 6" " registration on TRENCH A9b 60.59.	
		4.25 to 4.50 PM.	5 " 6" " on TRENCH A9b 60.57. } In retaliation to hostile TM. fire	
			6 " 6" " " MG A9b 60.55. }	
			5 " 6" " " hostile TM. DOVE }	
		4.30 to 5.15 PM.	10 " 6" " " " " DELL do. do.	JHK
	9th	8.40 to 10.40 AM.	21 " 2" " " " " DOVE In retaliation. enemy silenced.	
		12.40 to 4.40 PM	40 " 6" " " " " CAPE. CART. CAD. & T.M. at A22 a 79.94 } neutralization	
			5 - 2" " " " " at A16 c 6.5 }	
		~~9.15 PM.~~ 20 PM.	10 " 9.45" " " " " DELL.	"
		9.15 PM	5 " 6" " " " " CAD in retaliation.	JHK
	10th	7 to 8 AM.	10 " 6" " " " " FADE - -	
		10.45 -	5 " 6" " " " " A22 a 79.94. -	
		2.15 PM.	5 - 6" " " " " CAD "	
		3 to 4.30.	16 " 6" " " " " FADE & suspected TM at A9b 8 9. in retaliation	JHK
			5 " 2" " " " " Suspected TM. A10 c. 1.8 -	

CONTINUED ÷

(A7092). Wt W12839/M1293 75,0,0. 1/17. D. D. & L., Ltd. Forms/C.2118/14.

Instructions regarding War Diaries and Intelligence Summaries are contained in F. S. Regs., Part II. and the Staff Manual respectively. Title pages will be prepared in manuscript.

WAR DIARY or ~~INTELLIGENCE SUMMARY.~~

42nd TRENCH MORTARS R.A.

(Erase heading not required.)

Army Form C. 2118.

VOL X CONTINUED.

Place	Date	Hour	Summary of Events and Information	Remarks and references to Appendices
LE PREOL.	JANUARY 1918.			
	11th	8.30 am.	5 rds 6" bombs fired on hostile T.M. CAD in retaliation.	
		11.40	10 " 6" " " " " DEAR. DUCK DEEP. DEAN.	
		2.15 to 4.0 pm.	59 " 6" " " " TRENCHES & TMs at A10c11.80 & DEEP in retaliation	
			16 " 2" " " " " A9d94.65 A3D77.04 A10a25.70 in "	
		2.30 to 5.0 pm.	40 " 6" " " " " T.Ms CAD CAPE DOVE DAME DELL & TM at A16.c.60.50	
			10 " 9.45" " " " " " DAME. DOVE. DELL. in retaliation	JHWh
	12th	10 am to 10.30	15 " 6" " " " " " CAD & CART in retaliation	
		1.55 to 2.20 pm.	12 " 6" " " " " " DOVE & TRENCHES A10a25.70 & A10c60.66.	
			1 " 2" " " " TRENCH MORTAR & MG. A10c11.80.	
		3.0 to 4.30 pm.	18 " 6" " " " TRENCHES A10a25.70 A10c60.66. A9b65.60	
			1 " 2" " " " A10c40.58 A9c68.60 & T.M. A10c11.80 in retaliation	
			→ TRENCH A10c10.67.	
		2.0 pm.	4 " 2" " BRICKSTACKS A22.a.5.8 in retaliation	
		2.45 to 6 pm.	62 " 6" " " T.Ms DAY DAME DELL CAD CAP CAM CALL "	
		2.20 to 5.15 pm.	28 " 9.45" " " " DEER DUCK DELL DAME. "	JHWh
	13th	11 am	5 " 6" " " " " CAD "	
		1 to 4 pm.	13 " 6" " " " " DAME DELL. CAD "	
			2 " 9.45" " " " " POP "	

CONTINUED.

(A7092). Wt. W12839/M1293. 750,000. 1/17. D. D. & L., Ltd. Forms/C.2118/14.

Instructions regarding War Diaries and Intelligence Summaries are contained in F. S. Regs., Part II. and the Staff Manual respectively. Title pages will be prepared in manuscript.

WAR DIARY or ~~INTELLIGENCE SUMMARY.~~ 42ND TRENCH MORTARS R.A.

(Erase heading not required.)

VOL. X. CONTINUED.

Army Form C. 2118.

Place	Date	Hour	Summary of Events and Information	Remarks and references to Appendices
LE PREOL.	JANUARY 1918.			
	13th	4.30 PM.	16 rds 6" bombs fired on Trenches A9 b. 68. 60. A10 C 60.66 in retaliation to hostile T.M. fire.	
		10 PM.	5 " 6" " " " T.M. CAD	"
	14th	12.30	41 " 6" " " " CAP. CAM. CALL. CAD.	"
			5 " 9.45" " " " CAP CAM CALL	"
		3.15	3 " 9.45" " " " CAP CAM CALL	"
		6.30	2 " 9.45 " " " CAM.	"
		7.15	9 " 6" " " " A9 b 70.55 4 TRENCH A10 C 40.58	"
		3.10 to 6.30 PM	46 " 6" " " " DEEP CAD CART. CAPE	"
	15th	12.5 Am.	22 " 6" " " " DANE. DELL DAME.	
		10.5 Am.	5" 9.45" " " " RAILWAY EMBANKMENT A22 b. 7 9 SPOTTED DOG 4 T.M. DELL.	"
		1.30 PM.	18 " 6" " " " CAD in neutralization of hostile T.M. fire.	
		5.15	18 " 6" " " " CAD – – – – –	
	16th	10.10 Am	10 " 6" " " " CAM – – – – –	
	17th	10.10 Am	10 " 6" " " " CAM – – – – –	
		11.15 to 12.35 PM.	16 " 9.45" " " " DELL + DAME – – – –	
		12.35 to 12.50 PM.	33 " 6" " " " CALL – – – – –	

CONTINUED.

(A7092). Wt. W12839/M1293. 75,0.0. 1/17. D. D. & L., Ltd. Forms/C.2118/14.

Instructions regarding War Diaries and Intelligence Summaries are contained in F. S. Regs., Part II. and the Staff Manual respectively. Title pages will be prepared in manuscript.

WAR DIARY or ~~INTELLIGENCE SUMMARY.~~

(Erase heading not required.)

42nd TRENCH MORTARS RA.

Army Form C. 2118.

VOL. X CONTINUED.

Place	Date	Hour	Summary of Events and Information	Remarks and references to Appendices
LE PREOL.	18/1/18	8.20 to 9.30 AM.	15 rds 6" bombs fired on T.Ms. DAME. DELL. CAP. CAM. CALL. In neutralization of	
		10.25 to 10.30 –	20 – 6" " " " " CART & TM. A22 a 79.94 hostile TMs.	
		10.30 am.	5 – 6" " " " DOVE In retaliation for Granatenwerfers	
		7.45 to 8.15 PM.	15 – 6" " " " DOVE & A10. c11.80. Retaliation for granatenwerfer bombardment	
		12.45 PM.	10 – 6" " " " CAD CALL in retaliation for hostile TM fire.	
		11.50 to 2.30 PM.	32 – 9.45 " " registration on S.O.S. & TM. DEEP DELL & DAME	J. Hil[illegible]
	19th	8.15 to 10 am.	15 " 6" " " on TM CAD. in retaliation	
			6 " 9.45" " " " DEE & PIN –	
			10 9.45" " " " CAP. CAM. CALL & suspected TMs at A22 a & b.	
		12 noon to 1.15 PM.	26 " 9.45" " " registration with aeroplane observation on TM POP & PAD Several direct hits reported.	
		1.15 to 2 PM.	20 " 6" " registration with aeroplane observation on A22 a 75.65 & A22 a 85.68. Direct hits obtained	
		3.20 PM.	20 " 6" " " on TMs CAD. CALL in neutralization	
		4.25.	10 " 9.45" " " " CAP. CAM. CALL – –	[illegible]
	20th	7.15 to 8.50 am.	10 " 6" " " " CAM DEEP –	
			6 " 9.45" " " " CALL. DAY. DAM. –	
		11.15 am to 12 noon	9 " 9.45" " in vicinity of A4 a 4.9 –	
		3.30 PM	3 " 9.45" " on TM CAM.	[illegible]

CONTINUED

(A7092). Wt. W12839/M1293. 75,0.0. 1/17. D. D. & L., Ltd. Forms/C.2118/14.

Instructions regarding War Diaries and Intelligence Summaries are contained in F. S. Regs., Part II. and the Staff Manual respectively. Title pages will be prepared in manuscript.

WAR DIARY or ~~INTELLIGENCE SUMMARY.~~ 42ND TRENCH MORTARS R.A.

(Erase heading not required.)

VOL X CONTINUED.

Army Form C. 2118.

Place	Date	Hour	Summary of Events and Information	Remarks and references to Appendices
LE PREOL	20/1/18	1.30 PM.	5 rds 6" bombs fired on T.M CAM in neutralization.	
		12.30	10 - 6" " " " " CAD -	
		2.00	5 - 6" " " " DOVE -	
		3.50	20 - 6" " " in vicinity of A9 b 70.75 in neutralization of hostile TM fire	JHh
	21st	7.15am & 8.15am.	20 - 6" " " on TMs DEER DUCK DEEP CAD CAM -	
			20 - 6" " " " DOVE & TMs A10 C11.80. A9 b 75.90.	
		12.00 PM	4 - 9.45" " " AUCHY. DIAMOND DOOR COTTAGE.	
		12.15	5 - 6" " " TM CAPE neutralization	
		2.30	15 - 6" " " " DOVE & TM at A10 C11 80 in retaliation for Spring Bomb.	
		2.55	3 9.45 " " A10 C 9 6. A10 D 3 4. -	JHh
	22nd	12.30 PM.	5 - 9.45" " " " " POP in retaliation	
		2.0 PM	21 - 6" " " " DOVE & TM at A9 b 70.75 & TRENCH A10 C 40 58 in retaliation	
		3.20	1 - 9.45" " " " DEER	
		5.0	15 - 6" " " " DOVE. FADE & TM at A10 C 11 80.	JHh
	23rd	10.15	10 - 6" " " " CAM & CAD in neutralization	
		11.30 AM	2 - 9.45" " " " DEEP. -	
		2.15 PM	5 - 6" " " " CAB -	
		3.0	6 - 6" TRENCH A16 a 42 70. A10 a 12 20 Registration	
		4.15	35 - 6" " " TMs CAD CAPE CAM CALL CAP. Neutralization	
		4.45.	5 - 9.45" " " - DAM. -	JHh

CONTINUED.

(A7092). Wt W12839/M1293 75,000 1/17. D. D. & L., Ltd. Forms/C.2118/14.

Army Form C. 2118.

Instructions regarding War Diaries and Intelligence Summaries are contained in F. S. Regs., Part II. and the Staff Manual respectively. Title pages will be prepared in manuscript.

WAR DIARY
or
~~INTELLIGENCE SUMMARY.~~

(Erase heading not required.)

42ND TRENCH MORTARS. R.A.

VOL X CONTINUED.

Place	Date	Hour	Summary of Events and Information	Remarks and references to Appendices
LE PREOL.	23.1.18.	4.20 PM to 4.50	20 rds 6" bombs fired on TMs. FADE DOVE & TM at A10.C11.80 & TRENCH A9 b 75.90. eNeutralization	
		8.0 PM.	5 " 6" " " " " CAB } In retaliation.	
		11.15.	10 " 6" " " " " CAD & CAM. } In retaliation.	
	23/24th	Midnight	3 " 9.45" " " " " DAM } In retaliation.	
	24/1/18.	11.15 am to 12.40 PM.	35 " 6" " " " " CAP. CAM. CALL CAD in neutralization of hostile TMs	
		1.30 to 2.30 PM.	19 " 6" " " " " DOVE & TM at A10 c 11.80. Trench A10 a 42.50 & A10 a 25.70.	
		1.40 PM.	5 " 6" " " " " CAD. } Neutralization of hostile T.MS.	
		2.40	10 " 6" " " " " CAM. }	
		3.15	2 " 6" " " " " DOVE. }	
		4.15	5 " 6" " " " " CAP. }	
		4.30	10 " 6" " " " " DOVE & TRENCH A10 a 25.70 }	
		4.0	1 " 9.45" " " " " DEEP. Registration.	
		11.20 am	1 " 9.45" " " " " CAP. Retaliation	
		1.45 PM.	12 " 9.45" " " " " RAILWAY TRUCKS A22 b 7.9 Destructive	
	25/1/18.	12.30 PM.	9 " 9.45" " " " " TM. DEEP. Destructive shoot with aeroplane observation. Several direct hits obtained	

CONTINUED.

(A7092). Wt W12839/M1293. 75,0.0. 1/17. D. D. & L., Ltd. Forms/C.2118/14.

Instructions regarding War Diaries and Intelligence Summaries are contained in F. S. Regs., Part II. and the Staff Manual respectively. Title pages will be prepared in manuscript.

Army Form C. 2118.

WAR DIARY or ~~INTELLIGENCE SUMMARY.~~

(Erase heading not required.)

42ND TRENCH MORTARS RA.

VOL X CONTINUED.

Place	Date	Hour	Summary of Events and Information	Remarks and references to Appendices
LE PREOL.	25/1/18	12.30 PM to 2.0 PM.	30 rds 6" bomb fired on TMs DOVE & A10C11 80. A10C 10 20 and TRENCH A10A 4550 In neutralization of hostile TMs.	
		3.40 to 4.20 PM.	20 rds 6" " " " " CAM CAP CALL CAPE - - -	
	26/1/18	9.40 am.	5 " 6" " " " " CAM - - -	
		4.45 PM.	5 " 6" " " " " CAM - - -	
	27/1/18	8.55 am to 10.20 am	46 " 6" " " " " CAD CAP. CALL DEEP. Duck CAPE in neutralization	
		9 am to 10.20 am	11 " 9.45" " " " " DELL CAM & RAILWAY TRUCKS A22 b 7.9. retaliation	
		9.30 to 10.10 am	45 " 6" " " " " DOVE & TM at A10C10 20. & TRENCHES A10C40.58 A10C 6066. A10A 25.70 in retaliation	
		4-0 PM	5 " 6" " " " " DEEP in neutralization of hostile TMs	
			5 " 9.45" " " " " CAM - - - - -	
		8.30 to 9 PM	6 " 6" " " " TRENCH A10C40 58. A10C52.70 in retaliation	
		8.35 PM.	5 " 6" " " " TM CAB in neutralization.	
		10.45 to 11.15 PM.	18 " 6" " " " TM DOVE & TRENCH A10C4058 in retaliation	
		11.10 PM	21 " 6" " " " " CAM. CALL DEEP in neutralization	
			3 " 9.45" " " " " DAM & SPOTTED DOG TRENCH A22 b.4.5	

CONTINUED.

(A7092). Wt. W12839/M1293. 75,0.0. 1/17. D. D. & L., Ltd. Forms/C.2118/14.

Instructions regarding War Diaries and Intelligence Summaries are contained in F. S. Regs., Part II. and the Staff Manual respectively. Title pages will be prepared in manuscript.

WAR DIARY or ~~INTELLIGENCE SUMMARY.~~

(Erase heading not required.)

42nd Div Trench Mortars R.A. VOL X. CONTINUED.

Army Form C. 2118.

Place	Date	Hour	Summary of Events and Information	Remarks and references to Appendices
LE PREOL	28/1/18	8.50am to 9.25am.	35 rds 6" bombs fired on T.M's. CAPE CALL CAP in neutralization of hostile TMs.	
		9.20am to 9.35am	5 " 9.45" " " " - DAM & SPOTTED DOG TRENCH A22 b 4.5.	
		9.45 to 10.45am.	9 " 6" " " " " at A10 c11 80 & TRENCHES. A4 c45 15. A10 c 60.66. "	
		1.55 Pm to 2.0 -	15 " 6" " " " " CAM. CAD at TM at A28 a 3.5 in retaliation	
		2.15 -	12 - 6" " " " LTM at A22 a 35.00 In retaliation 2 directs obtained & enemy silenced	
		2.30 PM	5 " 6" " " " CHATEAU ALLEY } Retaliation - in cooperation	JHLh
			5 " 6" " " " DOOK ALLEY. } with Field Artillery	
		1.15 Pm.	7 " 6" " " " DAM. Registration with aeroplane observation 1 direct hit (OK) reported.	
	29/1/18	12.50 Pm.	4 " 6" " " " TRENCH A22 a 80.00 in retaliation	
		7.30 PM	6 9.45" " TM DAY in neutralization of hostile TMs.	
		8.40 -	10 " 6" " " " CAD - - - -	JHLh
		9.0 Pm	3 " 6" " " " TRENCH A10 c 52 72 in retaliation.	
	30th	10.50 am to 12.35 Pm.	35 " 6" " " " Registration on S.O.S line.	
		11.0 am	4 " 9.45" " " " TM DELL with aeroplane observation	JHLh

CONTINUED.

(A7092). Wt. W12839/M1293. 75,0 0 0. 1/17. D. D. & L., Ltd. Forms/C.2118/14.

Instructions regarding War Diaries and Intelligence Summaries are contained in F. S. Regs., Part II. and the Staff Manual respectively. Title pages will be prepared in manuscript.

WAR DIARY
or
~~INTELLIGENCE SUMMARY.~~
(Erase heading not required.)

42nd DIV TRENCH MORTARS R.A.
VOL X CONTINUED.

Army Form C. 2118.

Place	Date	Hour	Summary of Events and Information	Remarks and references to Appendices
LE PREOL.	30/1/18	12.35 PM.	8 rounds 6" bombs fired on Enemy Aeroplane which crashed in NO MANS LAND A16 a 4 4. a direct hit was obtained.	
		1.10 to 2.15 PM.	17 " 6" " " " TM DOVE & TRENCH SYSTEMS A10 c 40 58 A 3 d 77.04 in retaliation to hostile L.T.M. fire.	
		2.30 PM.	6 " 9.45" " " " A16 c 80.50 registration.	HhL
		3.0 PM	12 " 9.45" " " " RAILWAY TRUCKS at A16 d 25.12. 2 trucks were derailed & small ammunition dump blown up.	
	31st	3to 9.40 am.	10 " 6" " " " TM CAD in neutralization of hostile TMs.	
		1.45 PM to 3.50 PM.	35 " 6" " " " " CAM. CAPE. DUCK – – –	
		3.45 PM.	3 " 9.45" " " " " DEEP. – – –	HhL
		3.30 to 4.15 PM.	11 " 6" " " " " DOVE & A10 c 04.85 A 3 d 77.04 in retaliation to granatenwerfers.	

J. Hesketh[?]
Capt RFA
DTMO
42/Division

(A7092). Wt. W12839/M1293. 750.000. 1/17. D. D. & L., Ltd. Forms/C.2118/14.

CONFIDENTIAL.

Vol 12

WAR DIARY

of.

42ND DIV. TRENCH MORTARS. R.A.

FROM 1. 2. 1918.

To. 28. 2. 1918.

VOL. XI.

Instructions regarding War Diaries and Intelligence Summaries are contained in F. S. Regs., Part II. and the Staff Manual respectively. Title pages will be prepared in manuscript.

WAR DIARY or ~~INTELLIGENCE SUMMARY.~~

(Erase heading not required.)

42nd DIV TRENCH MORTARS RA.

FEBRUARY 1918.

Army Form C. 2118.

Place	Date	Hour	Summary of Events and Information	Remarks and references to Appendices
	FEBRUARY		1918. VOL XI.	
LE PREOL	2ND	11 am to 3.30 PM	45 rounds 6" bombs fired on TMs FADE, DOVE TM at A10 c11 80. CAP CAM. CALL	All
Headquarters			5 " 9.45" " " " DAM. All in neutralization of hostile TMs.	Coordinates
F10 b 5 2.	3rd		LT C. ELLIS and 28 ORs V 42 TMB transferred to form 1st Corps HTMs in	LA BASSEE
Bethune			accordance with 1st Army No 1569 G.	Map
Combined Sheet			3 Long Heavy TMs 9.45" Mark III handed over to 1st Corps. H.T.M.B.	1:10.000.
36a SE 36 SW			Medium T.M. Batteries reorganised in accordance with 1st Army No 1569 G i.e.	
36c NE 36c NW			2 Batteries "X" & "Y" composed of 4 Officers & 53 ORs to each.	
1: 40000	3rd	6.15 am	3 rounds 6" bombs fired on SUNKEN ROAD TRENCH in retaliation	
		12.30 PM	20 " 6" " " on TM A22 c 70.30 registration with aeroplane observation.	
			5 direct hits were obtained.	
		1.50 PM	5 rounds 6" bombs fired on TM. CAD in retaliation. during this shoot	
			a premature occurred, 3 ORs seriously wounded – 2 of whom since died –	
			& the gun & emplacement destroyed.	
		3.45 PM	14 rounds 6" bombs fired on TM DOVE A10 c11 80 + SUNKEN ROAD TRENCH in retaliation	
		5 PM	5 " 6" – – – – CAD –	
		6.15 PM	12 – 6" " " DOVE & TM at A9 b 75.90. – –	
			9 Medium T.Ms put in position to cover VILLAGE LINE.	

Continued

T2134. Wt. W708—776. 500000. 4/15. Sir J. C. & S.

Instructions regarding War Diaries and Intelligence Summaries are contained in F. S. Regs., Part II. and the Staff Manual respectively. Title pages will be prepared in manuscript.

Army Form C. 2118.

WAR DIARY or ~~INTELLIGENCE~~ SUMMARY.

(Erase heading not required.)

42nd Div TRENCH MORTARS RA.

FEBY 1918

Place	Date	Hour	Summary of Events and Information	Remarks and references to Appendices
			VOL XI CONTINUED.	
LE PREOL.	4/2/18	8.5am to 8.50am.	13 rounds 6" bombs fired on TMs DOVE A10c 41 80. A9 b 75 90 & MACKENSEN TRENCH in neutralization of hostile TMs.	
		3.30PM.	20 rounds 6" bombs fired on TM A22 a 79 94 with aeroplane registration (1 OK. & 4 Ys reported).	
		4 PM.	20 rounds 6" bombs fired on BRICKBAT ALLEY A22 a 75 42 with aeroplane observation. 5 direct hits reported.	gHth
	5th.	9.30am to 3.45PM	18 rounds 6" bombs fired on TMs DOVE & CAM in retaliation	gHth
	6th.	8.30 to Midnight	During this period 139 Bombs 6" on TMs DEEP CAP CAM CALL FADE DOVE DEER & MACKENSEN TRENCH in retaliation	
			11 Medium TMs 2" put in position to cover VILLAGE LINE	gHth
	7th.	12.10 to 12.45PM.	35 rounds 6" bombs fired on TMs CAD CAP CAM CALL & TRENCH A10 c 80.10	gHth
	8th.	11.45am to	15 " 6" " " " " CAD in retaliation.	
		12.45PM.	46 " 6" " " " " TMs DOVE. A9 b 75 90 & TRENCH A10 c 60 66 in retaliation	
		12.45 to 4PM.		
		2 to 4.30.	48 " 6" " " wire A16 a 35 70. Gap 15 yards wide cut.	gHth
			CONTINUED.	

T2134. Wt. W708—776. 500000. 4/15. Sir J. C. & S.

Instructions regarding War Diaries and Intelligence Summaries are contained in F. S. Regs., Part II. and the Staff Manual respectively. Title pages will be prepared in manuscript.

WAR DIARY or ~~INTELLIGENCE SUMMARY.~~

(Erase heading not required.)

42nd Div Trench Mortars RA.

Feby 1918.

Army Form C. 2118.

Place	Date	Hour	Summary of Events and Information	Remarks and references to Appendices
			VOL XI CONTINUED.	
LE PREOL	9/2/18	1.45 to 3 PM.	84 rounds 6" bombs fired on TRENCH A10 c 40.58 A16 a 35.70 A3 b 30.00 in retaliation & wire cutting.	JHth
		2.30 PM to 2.50 PM.	15 rounds 6" bombs fired to TMs CAP & CAPE in retaliation.	
	10/2/18	1.45 PM	10 " 6" " on TRENCH A10 c 60.66 A10 c 40.58 in retaliation	JHth
		11.45 am to 3.15 PM.	17 " 6" " " " CALL CAPE & DELL in retaliation	
	11th	7.45 to 11.45 am.	13 " 6" " " " TM DELL & TRENCH A9 b 70.75 –	
		6 to 6.45 PM.	136 " 6" " " " SUNKEN ROAD TRENCH in cooperation with Artillery in preparation for raid on enemy trenches.	JHth
	12th	12.5 PM	7 rounds 6" bombs fired on SNIPERS POST A9 d 90.50. Destructive Shoot.	
		2.15 to 4.15 PM.	39 " 6" " " " TMs DAY CALL CAPE CAM – neutralization of hostile TMs	JHth
	14th	9.50 to 12.10 PM.	82 " 6" " " S.O.S lines, Slow rate of fire during hostile gas bombardment.	
		12.10 PM.	17 rounds 6" bombs fired on TM DOVE in neutralization.	JHth
		2.50 to 3 PM	10 " 6" " " CAD " –	
	15th		All guns & stores handed over to 55th Division	JHth
			Continued.	

T2134. Wt. W708—776. 500000. 4/15. Sir J. C. & S.

Instructions regarding War Diaries and Intelligence Summaries are contained in F. S. Regs., Part II. and the Staff Manual respectively. Title pages will be prepared in manuscript.

WAR DIARY or ~~INTELLIGENCE SUMMARY.~~ 42nd Div Trench Mortars R.A.

(Erase heading not required.)

Army Form C. 2118.

FEBY 1918.

Place	Date	Hour	Summary of Events and Information	Remarks and references to Appendices
			VOL XI CONTINUED.	
LE PREOL	16/2/18	8am	Brigade moves by Motor lorries to VENDIN LES BETHUNE E4 a 4.4.	[illegible]
VENDIN LES BETHUNE E4 a 4.4	17/2/18 to 28/2/18		Brigade engaged on Tactical & Recreational Training.	[illegible]
Bethune	19/2/18		2LT WILCOX C.G. granted 14 days leave UK.	[illegible]
Combined Sheet 1:40000.	20/2/18		8 ORs proceed on course 1st Army School of Mortars	[illegible]
			8 - - - - 1st Corps Mine School.	
	27.2.18		9 - (Surplus to establishment) posted 42nd D.A.C.	[illegible]

[illegible]
Capt R.F.A.
D.T.M.O.
42/ Division

T2134. Wt. W708—776. 500000. 4/15. Sir J. C. & S.

42nd Divisional Artillery.

D. T. M. O.

42nd DIVISIONAL TRENCH MORTARS.

MARCH 1 9 1 8

Vol 13

CONFIDENTIAL

WAR DIARY

of

42nd DIV TRENCH MORTARS R.A.

FROM 1st MARCH 1918.

To 31st MARCH 1918

VOL XIII

War Diary. 42nd Div. Trench Mortars R.A. Vol XIII.

Place.	Time.	
VENDIN LES BETHUNE,	March 1918.	
E 4. A.	1. 3. 1918.	Brigade engaged on Tactical & Recreational Training.
BETHUNE	2. 3. 1918.	2 Officers & 60 OR's attached for duty with 11th Division
(Combined Sheet.)	8. 3. 1918	2 " & 60 " rejoin from 11th Division.
1: 40,000.	8. 3. 1918	Brigade proceeds to 1st Army School of Mortars for short course of instruction on 6" NEWTON T.M.
	17 3 1918.	Brigade leaves 1st Army School of Mortars and entrains for GONNEHEM.
GONNEHEM. V18 C. 8. 4.	18 3 1918 to 22. 3. 1918.	Brigade engaged on Tactical & Recreational Training
	23. 3. 1918.	Brigade proceeds by Motor Lorries to AYETTE
	24 3 1918	" ~~retires from AYETTE~~ & proceeds to MONCHY au BOIS
		1 Motor lorry abandoned ~~during retirement~~ owing to breakdown
MONCHY au BOIS.	25 3 1918.	Brigade proceeds to GAUDIEMPRE.

Continued –

War Diary. 42nd Divisional Trench Mortars R.A. VOL XIII CONTINUED.

Place	Date & Time		
GAUDIEMPRE.	27.3.1918. to 31.3.1918.	Brigade engaged on Ammunition Dumps at GAUDIEMPRE.	[illegible]

[illegible signature]
Capt RFA
DTMO.
42/ Divn.

IV.Corps.
Third Army.

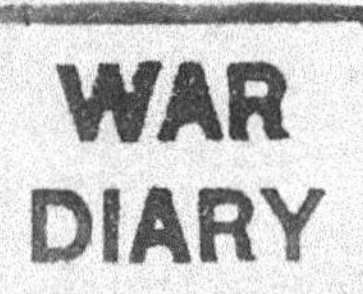

42nd DIVISION TRENCH MORTARS, R.A.

A P R I L

1 9 1 8

CONFIDENTIAL.

Vol 14

WAR DIARY

of

42nd DIVISION TRENCH MORTARS. R.A.

FROM 1. 4. 1918. To. 30. 4. 1918.

VOLUME XIII

Army Form C. 2118.

Instructions regarding War Diaries and Intelligence Summaries are contained in F. S. Regs., Part II. and the Staff Manual respectively. Title pages will be prepared in manuscript.

WAR DIARY 42ND. DIV TRENCH MORTARS R.A.
or
~~INTELLIGENCE SUMMARY.~~
(Erase heading not required.)

APRIL 1918.

Place	Date	Hour	Summary of Events and Information	Remarks and references to Appendices
	APRIL 1918		VOL. XIII.	
GAUDIEMPRE	1st.		Brigade engaged on Ammunition Dump at GAUDIEMPRE.	[illegible]
	2nd.		" moves to SOUASTRE.	[illegible]
SOUASTRE	3rd. to 5th.		" engaged on Ammunition Dump at SOUASTRE.	[illegible]
D15 d. 9.1.	3rd.		Positions reconnoitred for 2 NEWTON 6" at F19 a 90.40 Sheet 57D NE	
	5th.		Brigade moves to HANNESCAMPS.	[illegible]
HANNESCAMPS	6th.		Positions commenced at F19 a 90.40 (2)	[illegible]
E10 b 2.8.	8th.		Two extra positions commenced at F22 d 40.95 (2) "	[illegible]
Sheet 57D NE.	6th to 10th.		Work continued on positions.	[illegible]
	10th.		3 O.Rs killed 21 wounded by explosion of Ammunition Dump F22 Central.	
	11th.		Forward positions handed over to 62ND DIVISION.	[illegible]
	12th.		Reserve line reconnoitred for positions.	[illegible]
	13th.		Position commenced in Reserve line	[illegible]
	14th to 16th.		Work continued on positions in Reserve line.	[illegible]
	17th.	10am	Relieve 37th DIVISION on HEBUTERNE – FONQUEVILLERS SECTOR. 12 Mortars taken over	
Headquarters			in positions from 37th DIVISION ie; K16 a 25.50. K16 a 28.50. K10 c 95.70 (2 positions)	
COLIN J1 D 55.35			K9a 45.20 (2 positions). K10 b 95.90 (2) K6 c 95.95 (2) E28 c 60.10. E28 c 72.25.	[illegible]
			Continued:	

T2134. Wt. W708—776. 500000. 4/15. Sir J. C. & S.

Instructions regarding War Diaries and Intelligence Summaries are contained in F. S. Regs., Part II. and the Staff Manual respectively. Title pages will be prepared in manuscript.

WAR DIARY
or
~~INTELLIGENCE SUMMARY.~~
(Erase heading not required.)

42ND DIV: TRENCH MORTARS R.A.

Army Form C. 2118.

Place	Date	Hour	Summary of Events and Information	Remarks and references to Appendices
	APRIL 1918.		VOL XIII CONTINUED.	
COUIN	17 to 19th.		Detachments Stand-to. Usual fatigues in the line. Positions strengthened, &	
57 D 55-35.			ammunition taken to positions etc.	[initials]
	20th.		10 rounds 6" bombs fired on K17.C.6.9 and K17 C 6.4. registration.	[initials]
	Mid-night		funs at K16 a 25.50 (2) K9a 45.20 (2) taken over by N.Z. DIVISION for	[initials]
	23/24th.		tactical command – manned by personnel of 42nd DIV TRENCH MORTARS. –	
	25/30.		Work continued on fun positions & usual fatigues in the line.	[initials]

[signature]
Capt RFA
D.T.M.O.
42/Div

T2134. Wt. W708—776. 500000. 4/15. Sir J. C. & S.

CONFIDENTIAL.

Vol 15

WAR DIARY

of.

42ND. DIVISION TRENCH MORTARS. R. A.

FROM MAY 1ST 1918.

To. MAY 31ST. 1918.

VOLUME XIV.

Instructions regarding War Diaries and Intelligence Summaries are contained in F. S. Regs., Part II. and the Staff Manual respectively. Title pages will be prepared in manuscript.

WAR DIARY or ~~INTELLIGENCE SUMMARY.~~

(Erase heading not required.)

42ND DIV TRENCH MORTARS R.A.

Army Form C. 2118.

MAY 1918.

Place	Date	Hour	Summary of Events and Information	Remarks and references to Appendices
	MAY 1918.		VOL XIV.	
Headquarters	1st to		Detachment in the line. Work continued in strengthening positions, preparing	
COUIN	3rd.		alternative positions etc.	[initials]
J1 D 55.35	4th.	8.50 to 8.52 PM.	76 Rds 6" bombs fired on K17 a in conjunction with Artillery bombardment,	
Sheet 57D NE.			preparatory to attack by our Infantry.	[initials]
	6th.		41st Division T.M. take over left Divisional Front.	[initials]
	12th.		41st - - relieved by 57th Division – 42nd T.Ms under tactical administration	
			of 57th Division.	[initials]
			Right Divisional Front. 42nd T.M. positions as follows:–	
			K16 a 30.40. K16 a 32.40. K10 c 70.82 (2 guns) K9 a 50.50 (2 guns). Sheet 57D NE.	
	18th.		40 Rds 6" bombs fired on Suspected M.G. K17 c 05 65.	[initials]
	22nd.		15 " 6" " " " enemy post K17 a 05.60. Several direct hits obtained.	[initials]
	27th.	11 Am.	50 " 6" " " " hostile T.M. K17 c 20.50 } At request of Infantry.	[initials]
		1 PM	2 " 6" " " " O.P. K11 d 30.10. }	[initials]
	28th.	11.45 am	34 " 6" " " " enemy MG K16 d 70.30. Small fire started which burned for half an hour.	[initials]
		1.30 to 2 Pm	16 " 6" " " " Suspected TM K17 c 20.50 & registration on S.O.S lines K17 a 55.65.	
	31st	Midnight	6 Mortars. Right Divisional Front handed over to 57th Division	

[signature]
Capt R.F.A.
D.T.M.O. 42/Div.

T2134. Wt. W708—776. 500000. 4/15. Sir J. C. & S.

CONFIDENTIAL

Vol 16

WAR DIARY

of

42ND DIV TRENCH MORTARS. RA.

FROM 1. 6. 1918.

TO. 30. 6. 1918.

VOLUME XV.

Instructions regarding War Diaries and Intelligence Summaries are contained in F. S. Regs., Part II. and the Staff Manual respectively. Title pages will be prepared in manuscript.

WAR DIARY 42ND. TRENCH MORTARS. R.A. or ~~INTELLIGENCE SUMMARY.~~

(Erase heading not required.)

Army Form C. 2118.

JUNE 1918.

Place	Date	Hour	Summary of Events and Information	Remarks and references to Appendices
	JUNE 1918.		VOL. XV.	
Headquarters.		midnight 1st/2nd.	Relieve 37th Division (BUCQUOY SECTOR) and take over position as follows:-	
Couin			E30 b 72.85. E30 b 85.65. F26 d 75.15. F26 d 80.10. F26 d 95.05. F19 b 05.52. F19 b 10.55.	
T.1 d 55 35.			F20 c 95 40. F20 d 00.40 Sheet 57D NE. Under Tactical Administration 62nd Division.	[initials]
Sheet 57D NE.	4th	11.50 PM	40 rds 6" bombs fired on wire L2 d 94.30. and L3 c 07.20.	
			20 " 6" " " " Trench Junction L2 d 70.30.	
	4/5th	midnight	81 " 6" " " " L2 d 25.10 + L8 b 80.62	
			In accordance with instructions from Left Infantry Bde, 62nd Division, to cut wire for, and to support a raid on enemy's trenches.	[initials]
	8th	5 PM to 5.45 PM.	60 rds 6" fired on enemy T.Ms. L3 d 45.75. L3 d 70.65. L3 d 23.93. L3 c 35.05 in retaliation. enemy silenced.	
	9th.	11.45 AM.	50 rds 6" fired on hostile T.M. L9 a 50.95 in retaliation.	
			12 " 6" " " wire L2 d 20.10.	[initials]
			30 " 6" " " hostile T.Ms L3 d 20.85 and L3 d 45.70 in retaliation.	
	15th.	2.30 PM.	60 " 6" " " new work L3 d 75.75 and L3 c 85.28. Destructive fire.	[initials]
		3.30.	10 " 6" " " hostile T.M. L4 a 35.08.	[initials]
	17th.	12.30-3.30 PM.	50 " 6" " " " L3 d 22.95 destructive.	[initials]

CONTINUED:-

T2134. Wt. W708—776. 500000. 4/15. Sir J. C. & S.

Instructions regarding War Diaries and Intelligence Summaries are contained in F. S. Regs., Part II. and the Staff Manual respectively. Title pages will be prepared in manuscript.

WAR DIARY
or
~~INTELLIGENCE SUMMARY.~~
(Erase heading not required.)

42nd TRENCH MORTARS RA.

JUNE 1918.

Army Form C. 2118.

Place	Date	Hour	Summary of Events and Information	Remarks and references to Appendices
			VOL XV CONTINUED.	
	JUNE 1918			
Couin	17th.	12.30-3.30 Pm.	54 rds 6" fired on hostile T.M. L3 d 15.70. } Destructive.	[initials]
J1d 55.35.		4.20-5 Pm.	25 " 6" " enemy Post L3 b 50.05. }	[initials]
	18th.	6.20 Pm.	15 " 6" " " T.M. L3d 20.95 in retaliation	
	19th.	3 Pm to 4.30 Pm.	101 " 6" " " " L3d 17 85. L3 d 43.70 L3d 66.67 Destructive.	
	22/23rd	midnight.	60 " 6" " " " L3d 45.70. } Preparatory and to	[initials]
			60 " 6" " " " L3 d 68.67. } support a raid by our Infantry,	
			110 6" " " " L3d 65.97. } in accordance with 62nd Div Arty Order No 127.	
	26th.	10.30 am.	50 " 6" " " M.G. L.3 b 60 43. Destructive.	
	27th.	10.30 am	5 " 6" " " TM. L9 a 50 91 in retaliation	[initials]
		12.30 Pm.	35 " 6" " " " L3 d 66 67. Destructive	
		3.10 "	10 " 6" " " " L3 c 86.89 In retaliation.	
	28th.	6 to 6	25 " 6" " " " L8 to 6. L3d 66.67. L3 d 45.70 L9 a 50 91.	
		7.10 Pm.	in retaliation	
	29th.	12 noon.	Brigade moves to Bus & relieves N.Z Trench Mortars on Right Divisional Front - COLINCAMPS SECTOR - 12 mortars taken over in position.	[initials]
Bus. J26 d 55.85 Sheet 57D NE 1:20000.	30th	12 -	X Battery relieved on Left Divl Front - BUCQUOY Sector - by 37th & 57th Divisions.	
			CONTINUED :- PTO.	

T2134. Wt. W708—776. 500000. 4/15. Sir J. C. & S.

Instructions regarding War Diaries and Intelligence Summaries are contained in F. S. Regs., Part II. and the Staff Manual respectively. Title pages will be prepared in manuscript.

WAR DIARY
or
~~INTELLIGENCE SUMMARY.~~
(Erase heading not required.)

42nd Div Trench Mortars R.A.

June 1918

Army Form C. 2118.

Place	Date	Hour	Summary of Events and Information	Remarks and references to Appendices
	June 1918		VOL XV CONTINUED.	
Bus-les-Artois J26d 55.85 Sheet 57D NE	30/6/18	11 pm	Enemy Aircraft dropped 6 bombs on Bus les Artois J26d causing casualties to T.M. personnel. 4 killed & 17 severely wounded (O.Rs).	[initials]

[signature] for Capt RFA
DTMO
42/ Divn

T2134. Wt. W708—776. 500000. 4/15. Sir J. C. & S.

Confidential.

Vol 17

War Diary

— of —

42nd Divisional Trench Mortars, R.A.

From 1st July 1918. To 31st July 1918.

Volume XVI.

Instructions regarding War Diaries and Intelligence Summaries are contained in F. S. Regs., Part II. and the Staff Manual respectively. Title pages will be prepared in manuscript.

WAR DIARY
or
~~INTELLIGENCE SUMMARY.~~
(Erase heading not required.)

42ND DIV TRENCH MORTARS RA.

JULY 1918.

Army Form C. 2118.

Place	Date	Hour	Summary of Events and Information	Remarks and references to Appendices
	JULY 1918.		VOL. XVI	
BUS-LES-ARTOIS	1st	9am	15 rds 6" fired on T.M. K34.a 8.3. registration	HC
J26d 55.85		5PM	50 " 6" bombs " " ledge K28 a 4.4 to a1.8. Destructive	
1:20000		11.5PM to 11-30PM.	319 Rds 6" " in conjunction with Artillery - preparatory to a raid on enemy trenches by 1/8th Manchester.	
Sheet 57D NE.	2nd.	5am to 9.30am.	100 Rds 6" bombs fired on T.M. K34 a 8.3. Destructive	HC
	3rd	12 noon	40 " " " " " T.Ms. K22a K28a and c. registration	HC
		10PM	10 " " " " " T.M. K34 a 8.3 Destructive	
	4th.		During day 50 rds 6" bombs were fired on VALLADE and CHEEROH TRENCHES - destructive	HC
			96 " on BASIN WOOD, SACKVILLE ST and RED COTTAGE.	
			42 " on M.Gs K22a 20.55 K22a 70.59 and K22a 48.48	
	5th.		" " 180 " on Trenches K28c 15.15 to 15.10. K34a 18.92 to 20.70 K22a 22.50. K22a 25.22. K22c 26.90 K28c 18.18 to K34c 20.65. and K34a 8.3. - All destructive	HC
	6th.		80 rds 6" bombs fired on Enemy's New Trench K34a. QUARRY. K27 b 75.62 RED COTTAGE and M.G. K22 a 55.55 LYCEUM and VALLADE TRENCHES. - destructive	HC
		9 to 10PM.	65 rds 6" bombs were fired on Enemy Trenches from K22a to K28c in retaliation for shelling of our trenches.	

T2134. Wt. W708—776. 500000. 4/15. Sir J. C. & S.

CONTINUED :-

*Instructions regarding War Diaries and Intelligence Summaries are contained in F. S. Regs., Part II. and the Staff Manual respectively. Title pages will be prepared in manuscript.

WAR DIARY
or
~~INTELLIGENCE SUMMARY.~~
(Erase heading not required.)

42nd Divl TRENCH MORTARS RA.

JULY 1918.

Army Form C. 2118.

Place	Date	Hour	Summary of Events and Information	Remarks and references to Appendices
	July 1918.		VOL XVI CONTINUED.	
BUS-LES ARTOIS.	7th.		During day 110 rds 6" bombs were fired on LA SIGNY FARM. BASIN WOOD. K22a 55.20 & K22a 55.60. K34 Central - destructive -	OJH
	8th	2-3.30 AM.	Enemy bombarded COLINCAMPS and vicinity with Gas Shells.	OJH
		1.30-2.35 PM.	80 rds 6" bombs fired on enemy's NEW TRENCH K28c 15.05. Suspected O.P. K28c 40.40 & VALLADE TRENCH.	
		6.15 to 6.45 PM	118 rds 6" bombs fired on TRENCH (behind hedge) K28c 42.35. to K28c 15.75 and TRENCH K22c 27.55: K22a 25.05. All destructive.	
	9th.	4.20 AM	80 rds 6" bombs fired in retaliation on enemy trench K34 a. 60.40. 86 " 6" " " on trenches & trench Junctions K28c 1.2. K28a 40.65 to 40.45. K34 Central. K34 a 60.70 & K34d 27.80 Harassing and destructive fire.	OJH
	10th.	3.10 PM	52 rds 6" bombs fired on Enemy Post K34a 25.20. Direct hit obtained & sap running into trench destroyed.	OJH
		6 PM to midnight	75 rds 6" bombs fired on trenches and trench Junctions K28a 4.3 to 4.6 and BASIN WOOD. - destructive.	
	11th.	4.10 AM to 6.18 AM	20 rds 6" bombs fired on LYCEUM & Trench Junction K34a 84.38. Destructive.	OJH

CONTINUED.

T2134. Wt. W708—776. 500000. 4/15. Sir J. C. & S.

Instructions regarding War Diaries and Intelligence Summaries are contained in F. S. Regs., Part II. and the Staff Manual respectively. Title pages will be prepared in manuscript.

WAR DIARY
or
~~INTELLIGENCE SUMMARY.~~
(Erase heading not required.)

42nd Div TRENCH MORTARS R.A.

JULY 1918.

Army Form C. 2118.

Place	Date	Hour	Summary of Events and Information	Remarks and references to Appendices
	July 1918.		VOL XVI CONTINUED.	
BUSLES-ARTOIS.	11th	3PM to 4PM.	100 rds 6" bombs fired on Trenches K27b 99.70 to 99.55. K28c 30.30 to 25.25 and New Work K28c 1.2 to 2.1. Several direct hits obtained and large quantity of timber blown into the air.	[illegible]
	12th.	4 a.m to 5.40 a.m.	20 rds 6" bombs fired on LYCEUM & VALLADE TRENCHES. During the day 94 bombs 6" were fired on New Trench K28c.1.2, Trench K28c 00.33 to 00.66 M.Gun K34 d 2.7 – Destructive.	[illegible]
	13th		119 rds 6" bombs fired on Trenches K22c 27.85 to 24.96 K28 c.2.3. Trench Junctions K28 a 00.33 } K28 a 00.60 } BASIN WOOD. VALLADE and LYCEUM TRENCHES.	[illegible]
	14th.		100 rds 6" bombs fired on Trenches along ledge K28c and K27a and BORDEN AVENUE K34 d 40.95. – destructive –.	[illegible]
	15th.		45 rds 6" bombs fired on CHALK PIT K27. LA SIGOY FARM and enemy T.M. K34 Central – destructive.	[illegible]
	16th.		65 rds 6" bombs fired on SUNKEN ROAD K22a 9c.	
		4–9 PM	54 – 6" " " " BASIN WOOD & QUARRIES K28a 00.60.	[illegible]
		11.45 PM	25 " 6" " " " T.M. & TRENCHES K34 Central	

T2134. Wt. W708—776. 500000. 4/15. Sir J. C. & S.

CONTINUED:–

Instructions regarding War Diaries and Intelligence Summaries are contained in F. S. Regs., Part II. and the Staff Manual respectively. Title pages will be prepared in manuscript.

WAR DIARY or ~~INTELLIGENCE SUMMARY.~~

(Erase heading not required.)

42nd Div Trench Mortars RA.

JULY 1918.

Army Form C. 2118.

Place	Date	Hour	Summary of Events and Information	Remarks and references to Appendices
	JULY 1918		VOL XVI CONTINUED	
BUS-LES-ARTOIS	17th.	12.30am	10 rds 6" bombs fired on M.G. & Trenches K34a 8 3.	DJH
		4am/7.30am.	25 " 6" " " POST K27b 8.1.	
		11 am	20 " 6" " " " " K27b 8.1. K27 b 9.2. K28 c 0.9.	
		1.15PM	31 " 6" " " registration on Tunnel K34a 20.00 and Trench Junction K34 Central.	DJH
		4-6PM	120 rds 6" bombs fired on enemy TMs in K34 a and b in accordance with 42nd Div: Artillery Instructions No 19. Preparatory to raid on enemy post.	
	18th.	1.55am to 2.25am.	80 rds 6" bombs fired on K27 b 8.1. K27 b. 9.2 K28a 00.60 & SUNKEN ROAD K22a 20 40 in support of raid on enemy Trenches.	DJH
		9PM-11.30PM.	50 rds 6" bombs fired on K28c and TM. K34 Central	
	19th.	12.30am.	10 rds 6" " " " Trench Junction K34 a 8 3. } Destructive	DJH
		3 am	35 " 6" " " Trenches K28a } Destructive	
		11.52am	21 " 6" " " TM K35c registration.	
		1PM/to 20PM.	45 " 6" " " Trench K27 b 98.60 to 80.15 and Trench Junction K28 a 5.1.	

CONTINUED :-

T2134. Wt. W708—776. 500000. 4/15. Sir J. C. & S.

Instructions regarding War Diaries and Intelligence Summaries are contained in F. S. Regs., Part II. and the Staff Manual respectively. Title pages will be prepared in manuscript.

WAR DIARY
or
~~INTELLIGENCE SUMMARY.~~
(Erase heading not required.)

42nd Div. TRENCH MORTARS R.A.

Army Form C. 2118.

JULY 1918.

Place	Date	Hour	Summary of Events and Information	Remarks and references to Appendices
			VOL XVI CONTINUED.	
BUS-LES-ARTOIS.	July 1918 20th.	2.50 PM to 8 PM.	65 rds 6" bombs fired on T.M. K 35 c 65.65. BASIN WOOD and Trench Junction K28 a 5.1.	[illegible]
	21st	4.20 am to 6.20 am.	20 rds 6" bombs fired on VALLADE TRENCH and BORDEN AVENUE	[illegible]
		8.30 PM/10.30 PM	10 rds 6" bombs fired on Trench K28 a 85.60 and 85.35.	[illegible]
	22nd	2.45/4 am	10 rds 6" " " " " K28 a 85.60 " 85.35.	
		10/10.30 am	30 " 6" " " " K28 c 15.20 to BASIN WOOD.	
			50 " 6" " " " BASIN WOOD in support of our Infantry "pushing out" our line.	[illegible]
	23rd	3.30 PM	10 rds 6" bombs fired on T.M. K34 Central.	
	24th.	5.20 am	20 " 6" " " VALLADE TRENCH.	[illegible]
		12.5 PM to 1.45.	275 " 6" " " YALLADE TRENCH - ROMAN RD - from BORDEN AVENUE to MOUNTJOY TRENCH. 17 Rds 6" on T.M. K28 a 80.35 and SACKVILLE ST in conjunction with Artillery in bombardment on enemy trenches.	
		6.15 PM	25 rds 6" bombs fired on CHEEROH AVENUE and VALLADE TRENCH.	[illegible]

T2134. Wt. W708—776. 500000. 4/15. Sir J. C. & S.

CONTINUED

Instructions regarding War Diaries and Intelligence Summaries are contained in F. S. Regs., Part II. and the Staff Manual respectively. Title pages will be prepared in manuscript.

WAR DIARY
or
~~INTELLIGENCE SUMMARY.~~
(Erase heading not required.)

42ND DIV TRENCH MORTARS R.A.

Army Form C. 2118.

Place	Date	Hour	Summary of Events and Information	Remarks and references to Appendices
	July 1918		VOL XVI CONTINUED.	
BUS LES	25th	6.50 PM.	20 rds 6" bombs fired on K34 Central.	[illegible]
ARTOIS.	26th	3.30 am to 4.20 AM.	30 " 6" " " LYCEUM and CHEEROH AVENUE } Destructive.	[illegible]
	28th.	7.35 PM.	20 " 6" " " " TRENCH JUNCTION K34a 80.35. } Destructive.	[illegible]
	29th.	3.35 PM	35 " 6" " " " TUNNEL K34a 20.00. Much timber was blown into the air.	
	30th	9/10 am	160 " 6" " " " VALLADE TRENCH in accordance with 42nd Div Order No 25.	[illegible]
	31st		100 " 6" " " " VALLADE TRENCH. Trenches K34 b & d & K28a 80 40 to 70.35	[illegible]

S J Hayward
Capt R.F.A.
a/ D.T.M.O.
42/Div

T2134. Wt. W708—776. 500000. 4/15. Sir J. C. & S.

CONFIDIENTIAL

Vol 18

WAR DIARY

of.

42ND. DIVISION TRENCH MORTARS. RA.

FROM. 1ST AUGUST 1918.

TO. 31ST AUGUST. 1918.

VOLUME XVII.

Instructions regarding War Diaries and Intelligence Summaries are contained in F. S. Regs., Part II. and the Staff Manual respectively. Title pages will be prepared in manuscript.

WAR DIARY or ~~INTELLIGENCE SUMMARY.~~

(Erase heading not required.)

42ND DIV TRENCH MORTARS R.A.

AUGUST 1918.

Army Form C. 2118.

Place	Date	Hour	Summary of Events and Information	Remarks and references to Appendices
			VOL XVII	
	AUGUST 1918.			
BUS LES ARTOIS				
J26 d 55 85	1ST.	12.30 Pm	20 rds 6" bombs fired registration on OBSERVATION WOOD.	DC
1:20000	2ND	3.10 Pm.	100 " 6" " " on GREEN ST & LEGEND TRENCHES. } Destructive.	
Sheet 27 D NE		6 Pm	100 " 6" " " LEGEND TRENCH and vicinity K34a 2.2. }	
		10.40 Pm/11.55 Pm	16 " 6" " " on K28 b.3.3. Harassing.	
	3rd	7.30 am.	15 " 6" " " on K28 b.3.3 "	DC
		11.30 am/2.Pm.	105 " 6" " " on REDAN and OBSERVATION WOOD. Destructive.	
	4th.	11.55 am.	140 " 6" " " VALLADE, GREEN ST and CHEAPSIDE "	
		6 Pm.	120 " 6" " " TRENCHES vicinity of K34c5.9 and K34d2.3 Destructive.	
		1.15 Pm/9. Pm	140 " 6" " " BASIN and OBSERVATION WOODS. "	
	5th.	4 Pm	150 " 6" " " LEGEND and VALLADE TRENCHES and vicinity of K34d 20 55.	DC
			37 " 6" " " on BASIN WOOD	
	6th.	2 Pm	120 " 6" " " VALLADE TRENCH and Communication Trenches leading to WATLING ST	
		6/7 Pm	175 " 6" " " BASIN WOOD.	
	7th.	2.30 Pm	125 " 6" " " VALLADE TRENCH. TRENCHES K34a 2.0 b 3.4. & K34d 3.2.	DC
		5 / 6.55 Pm.	45 " 6" " " BASIN & OBSERVATION WOODS	
			25 " 6" " " Trenches K28 d 70.35 b K28 c 75 35.	

CONTINUED

T2134. Wt. W708—776. 500000. 4/15. Sir J. C. & S.

Instructions regarding War Diaries and Intelligence Summaries are contained in F. S. Regs., Part II. and the Staff Manual respectively. Title pages will be prepared in manuscript.

WAR DIARY
or
~~INTELLIGENCE SUMMARY.~~
(Erase heading not required.)

42ND Div TRENCH MORTARS RA.

AUGUST 1918.

Army Form C. 2118.

Place	Date	Hour	Summary of Events and Information	Remarks and references to Appendices
			VOL XVIII CONTINUED.	
	AUG 1918			
BUSLES	8th	9am/4PM.	110 rds 6" bombs fired on selected harassing targets in K34 b. c and d.	
ARTOIS.		5PM/9.30PM	50 " 6" " " OBSERVATION WOOD and trenches in rear and K34a 60 65.	PC
	9th.	4.30am.	20 " 6" " " K34 d 70 80.	
		9am/4PM.	160 " 6" " " K34 b c and d. and wire in front of VALLADE and WATLING ST. TRENCHES.	
		2.30/3.30PM.	77 rds 6" bombs fired on BASIN and OBSERVATION WOODS.	
	10th.	2.30PM	60 " 6" " " GREEN ST and REDAN	PC
			80 " 6" " " wire in front of WATLING ST.	
		4PM.	70 " 6" " " OBSERVATION WOOD.	
	11th	3PM	75 " 6" " " Vicinity K34 d 3.2 at request of infantry.	
		6/7PM	105 " 6" " " TRENCH AVENUE K28c 90.45 to JUNCTION of LEGEND and to K28d 15 30.	
	12th.	1.30/2.30PM.	50 rds 6" fired on OBSERVATION WOOD.	PC
		6/6.30PM	20 " 6" " " enemy post K28 central.	
	13th.	3/4PM.	150 " 6" " " selected harassing target in K34 b. c and d	
		10.30/11.30PM.	40 " 6" " " Trench from K28 central to OBSERVATION WOOD	

CONTINUED –

Instructions regarding War Diaries and Intelligence Summaries are contained in F. S. Regs., Part II. and the Staff Manual respectively. Title pages will be prepared in manuscript.

WAR DIARY or ~~INTELLIGENCE SUMMARY.~~

(*Erase heading not required.*)

42ND DIV TRENCH MORTARS RA.

AUGUST 1918.

Army Form C. 2118.

Place	Date	Hour	Summary of Events and Information	Remarks and references to Appendices
	Aug 1918.		VOL XVIII Continued.	
Bus LES ARTOIS.	14th	4/6 am.	30 rds 6" bombs fired on Trench K28 Central to OBSERVATION WOOD.	[initials]
	15th		Germans withdraw from trenches - putting all guns out of action.	
	19th		1 Officer attached to 210th Bde and 1 to 211th Bde for duty.	
			40 ORs attached to 42nd Div A.R.P. for duty.	
	20th		6 " " to 42nd Div Signals for duty.	
	28th.		Remainder of Brigade proceeds to MIRAUMONT.	
MIRAUMONT	29/30th		Engaged on various fatigues.	

[signature] Capt RFA
for DTMO.
42 Div

T2134. Wt. W708—776. 500000. 4/15. Sir J. C. & S.

CONFIDENTIAL.

Vol 19

WAR DIARY

OF.

42ND DIV: TRENCH. MORTARS. R.A.

FROM. 1. 9. 1918.

TO. 30. 9. 1918.

VOLUME XVIII.

Instructions regarding War Diaries and Intelligence Summaries are contained in F. S. Regs., Part II. and the Staff Manual respectively. Title pages will be prepared in manuscript.

WAR DIARY
or
~~INTELLIGENCE SUMMARY.~~
(Erase heading not required.)

42ND DIV TRENCH MORTARS R.A.

SEPTEMBER 1918.

Army Form C. 2118.

Place	Date	Hour	Summary of Events and Information	Remarks and references to Appendices
	SEPT. 1918		VOL XVIII	
MIRAUMONT	1st.		Proceed to GREVILLERS. Two Newton T.Ms. and two light German Minenwerfers taken into action by Tank.	[initials]
GREVILLERS	2ND.	2am/3.30am	10½ Bombs 6" and 200 Minenwerfer bombs fired on VILLERS-AU-FLOS and NORTHERN & SOUTHERN Outskirts, preparatory to Infantry attack.	[initials]
	3rd.		Move forward by road march to RIENCOURT N4.C.5.9. Fatigues on Ammunition Dumps etc.	[initials]
RIENCOURT.	4th.		Proceed by road march to BARASTRE O15 a 70.25.	[initials]
BARASTRE O15.a 70.25	4/21st.		Fatigues on Ammunition Dumps etc.	
Sheet 57.C.	11th.		2LT. CARRICK J.D. 2/42TMB & 1 O.R. attached B/210 for duty.	[initials]
	11th.		2LT CARRICK J.D. - Killed in action.	[initials]
			2LT. COLLINS S.H - Wounded in action.	[initials]
	21st.		Relieve 37th Division T.Ms. Brigade proceeds by road march to RUYAULCOURT.	[initials]
RUYAULCOURT P10 d 05 50 Sheet 57C.	22nd	12	T.M. Positions commenced at Q4d 05 95. Q4b 05 05. Q4a 78.62 Q4a 78.68 Q4a 77.75 Q4a 77 79. ("X" Battery) Q4d 43.52. Q4d 45.53. Q4d 45 55. Q4d 35 80. Q4d 22.80 (2) ("Y" Battery).	[initials]

CONTINUED

T2134. Wt. W708—776. 500000. 4/15. Sir J. C. & S.

Instructions regarding War Diaries and Intelligence Summaries are contained in F. S. Regs., Part II. and the Staff Manual respectively. Title pages will be prepared in manuscript.

WAR DIARY
or
~~INTELLIGENCE SUMMARY.~~
(Erase heading not required.)

42ND DIV TRENCH MORTARS RA.

SEPTEMBER. 1918.

Army Form C. 2118.

Place	Date	Hour	Summary of Events and Information	Remarks and references to Appendices
			VOL XVIII CONTINUED	
RUYAULCOURT.	27.9.18.	7.52am/8.30am.	518 rds 6" bombs fired on selected targets preparatory to	[illegible]
P.10.d.05.50			Infantry attack in accordance with 42nd Div Arty Instructions No 36.	
Sheet 57C.	28/30th.		General routine.	

[signature]

Capt RFA
D.T.M.O
42nd Div.

T2134. Wt. W708—776. 500000. 4/15. Sir J. C. & S.

CONFIDENTIAL.

Vol 20

WAR DIARY

— of —

42nd DIVISIONAL TRENCH MORTARS R.A.

FROM 1st OCTOBER 1918. 31st OCTOBER 1918.

VOLUME XIX.

Instructions regarding War Diaries and Intelligence Summaries are contained in F. S. Regs., Part II. and the Staff Manual respectively. Title pages will be prepared in manuscript.

WAR DIARY or ~~INTELLIGENCE SUMMARY.~~

(Erase heading not required.)

42ND DIV. TRENCH MORTARS R.A.

OCTOBER 1918.

Army Form C. 2118.

Place	Date	Hour	Summary of Events and Information	Remarks and references to Appendices
	Oct 1918.			
RUYAULCOURT P10d 05 50 Sheet 57 c.	2.10.18.		Move forward by road march to TRESCAULT.	HLh
TRESCAULT Q4a 76 50.	3.10.18 to 10.10.18.		Engaged on re-fitting and general routine.	HLh
	10.10.18		Proceed by road march to LESDAIN N2 b.0.8.	HLh
LESDAIN N2b.0.8 Sheet 57 B.	11.10.18		Proceed by road march to BEAUVOIS-EN-CAMBRESIS.	HLh
BEAUVOIS EN CAMBRESIS. I9.d.3.3.	12.10.18		Positions reconnoitred at D.24.c	HLh
	13.10.18		Two 6" Mortars taken into action at D 24 c 65.40.	HLh
		8.30p	100 rounds 6" Bombs fired on Railway Embankment and Roads vicinity E 13 c 80.50.	HLh

T2134. Wt. W708–776. 500000. 4/15. Sir J. C. & S.

Army Form C. 2118.

Instructions regarding War Diaries and Intelligence Summaries are contained in F. S. Regs., Part II. and the Staff Manual respectively. Title pages will be prepared in manuscript.

WAR DIARY or ~~INTELLIGENCE~~ SUMMARY.

(*Erase heading not required.*)

42/DIVL. TRENCH MORTARS R.A.

October 1918.

Place	Date	Hour	Summary of Events and Information	Remarks and references to Appendices
	Oct 1918			
BEAUVOIS	15.10.18		Proceed by road march to BEAUVOIS I 11 b 50.05.	Hhh
			a/Capt. J. A. F. MACNAIR, R.F.A. (T.F.) admitted to Hospital sick	
BEAUVOIS I 11 b. 50.05 SHEET 54B	16.10.18		Proceed by road march to QUIEVY D19 b 85.25.	Hhh
QUIEVY D19 b 85.25. SHEET 54B	17.10.18		New Zealand Trench Mortar Batteries attached for tactical administration.	
			Positions reconnoitred at D18a (Sheet 54 B. NE)	
			Work commenced on ten positions at D18a 45.30. D18a 40.38. D18a 68.40. D18a 65.45. D18a 60.50. (X & Y Batteries). D18a 60.20. D18a 55.20. D18a 50.20. D18a 50.25. D18a 55.25 (New Zealand T. M. Batteries).	Hhh
	18.10.18		Work continued on Positions.	Hhh
	19.10.18		Positions completed – ammunition taken to positions.	
	20.10.18	2.0 am to 2.45 am	40 rounds 6" fired on FACTORY E13a	Hhh
			650 " " " " RAILWAY E13 b 0.6. – E4 c 2.4.	
	22.10.18		Proceed by road march to BRIASTRE D.24 c 85.30.	Hhh

D. D. & L., London, E.C. (A7883) Wt. W603/M1672 350,000 4/17 Sch. 52a Forms/C/2118/14

Instructions regarding War Diaries and Intelligence Summaries are contained in F. S. Regs., Part II. and the Staff Manual respectively. Title pages will be prepared in manuscript.

WAR DIARY ~~or~~ ~~INTELLIGENCE SUMMARY.~~

(Erase heading not required.)

Army Form C. 2118.

42/DIVL TRENCH MORTARS R.A.

October 1918

Place	Date	Hour	Summary of Events and Information	Remarks and references to Appendices
	Oct 1918			
BRIASTRE D24c 85.30. SHEET 57B.	22.10.18		Positions reconnoitred at W. 26 a 95.25.	
			Position completed - Ammunition carried to position	HHH
			One gun taken into action	
			Charges destroyed by enemy shell fire	
	23.10.18		Proceed by road march to SOLESMES D12 b 50.80.	HHH
SOLESMES D12 b 50.80	25.10.18		Proceed by road march to SOLESMES D24c 80.80.	HHH
	24.10.18		Proceed by road march to ROMERIES W21 b 95.15.	
ROMERIES W21 b 95.15 SHEET 51A SE	24.10.18 - 31.10.18		X and Y Batteries engaged on fatigues for 42/D.A.C.	HHH

H. Hewitt. Capt
D.T.M.O. 42 Division.

D. D. & L., London, E.C. (A7883) Wt. W803/M1672 350,000 4/17 Sch. 52a Forms/C/2118/14

CONFIDENTIAL.

VR 21

WAR. DIARY

of

42ND. DIV: TRENCH MORTARS. R.A.

FROM. 1. 11. 1918.

TO. 30. 11. 1918.

VOLUME XX.

Instructions regarding War Diaries and Intelligence Summaries are contained in F. S. Regs., Part II. and the Staff Manual respectively. Title pages will be prepared in manuscript.

WAR DIARY
or
~~INTELLIGENCE SUMMARY.~~
(Erase heading not required.)

42ND DIV TRENCH MORTARS RA

NOVEMBER 1918.

Army Form C. 2118.

Place	Date	Hour	Summary of Events and Information	Remarks and references to Appendices
			VOL XX.	
ROMERIES	1st to		Engaged on fatigues with 42ND D.A.C.	[initials]
W.21.b.95.15	5th			
Sheet 51A SE	6th		Proceed by road march to VILLEREAU M28 b 40.80.	[initials]
VILLEREAU	7th to		Engaged on fatigues for 42ND D.A.C.	[initials]
M28 b 40.80	11th			
Sheet 57.	12th		Proceed by road march to ~~Pont-Sur-Sambre~~. LA HAUTE RUE (PONT DE SAMBRE)	[initials]
PONT-SUR-	13th to		Engaged on fatigues & general training.	
SAMBRE.	30/11/1918.			
O33.c.7.2.				

[signature]

Capt RFA
D.T.M.O
42nd Div

T2134. Wt. W708–776. 500000. 4/15. Sir J. C. & S.

Instructions regarding War Diaries and Intelligence Summaries are contained in F. S. Regs., Part II. and the Staff Manual respectively. Title pages will be prepared in manuscript.

WAR DIARY
or
INTELLIGENCE SUMMARY.
(Erase heading not required.)

42ND DIV TRENCH MORTARS RA

NOVEMBER 1918

Army Form C. 2118.

Place	Date	Hour	Summary of Events and Information	Remarks and references to Appendices
			VOL XX	
ROMERIES	1st		Engaged on fatigues with 42ND D.A.C	H.L.
W 21 b 95 15	5th			
Sheet 51A SE	6th		Proceed by road-march to VILLEREAU M28 b 40 80.	H.L.
VILLEREAU	7th		Engaged on fatigues for 42ND DAC	H.L.
M28 b 40 80	11th			
Sheet 51	12th		Proceed by road march to ~~Pont Sur Sambre~~ LA HAUTE RUE (PONT DE SAMBRE)	H.L.
PONT-SUR-SAMBRE	13th to 30/11/1918.		Engaged on fatigues + general training	
D33 c 7 2				

H. L. [signature]
Capt RFA
DTMO
42nd Div

T2134. Wt. W708—776. 500000. 4/15. Sir J. C. & S.

CONFIDENTIAL

WAR DIARY

OF

42ND DIV TRENCH MORTARS. RA.

FROM 1. 12. 1918.

TO 31ST. 12. 1918.

VOLUME XXI

Instructions regarding War Diaries and Intelligence Summaries are contained in F. S. Regs., Part II. and the Staff Manual respectively. Title pages will be prepared in manuscript.

WAR DIARY or ~~INTELLIGENCE SUMMARY.~~

Army Form C. 2118.

(Erase heading not required.)

42ND DIV TRENCH MORTARS. RA.

DECEMBER 1918.

Place	Date	Hour	Summary of Events and Information	Remarks and references to Appendices
	DECR. 1918		VOL XXI.	
LA HAUTE RUE	1/13.		Brigade engaged on fatigues for 42ND D.A.C and Recreational Training	
PONT-SUR-SAMBRE	14th.		Proceed by road-march to MARPENT.	
MARPENT.	15th		- - - - - LOBBES.	
LOBBES.	18th		- - - - - CHATELINEAU	
CHATELINEAU	19/31st.		Brigade engaged on fatigue for 42ND. D.A.C.	[signature]

[signature]

Capt R.F.A.

D.T.M.O.

42ND. Divn.

T2134. Wt. W708—776. 500000. 4/15. Sir J. C. & S.

VR 23

CONFIDENTIAL.

WAR DIARY

of.

42ND DIV TRENCH. MORTARS. R.A.

FROM. 1ST. JANUARY 1919

TO. 31ST. JANUARY 1919.

VOLUME. XXII

Instructions regarding War Diaries and Intelligence Summaries are contained in F. S. Regs., Part II. and the Staff Manual respectively. Title pages will be prepared in manuscript.

WAR DIARY
or
~~INTELLIGENCE~~ SUMMARY.
(Erase heading not required.)

42ND DIV: TRENCH. MORTARS. R.A.

JANUARY. 1919.

Army Form C. 2118.

Place	Date	Hour	Summary of Events and Information	Remarks and references to Appendices
	JANUARY 1919.		VOL XXII.	
CHATELINEAU	1ST to 31ST.		T.M. Personnel attached to 42ND. D.A.C. for duty.	
			A Rushton Lt. for D.T.M.O. 42ND Divn	

T2134. Wt. W708–776. 500000. 4/15. Sir J. C. & S.

www.ingramcontent.com/pod-product-compliance
Lightning Source LLC
Chambersburg PA
CBHW081545160426
43191CB00011B/1846
* 9 7 8 1 4 7 4 5 2 0 7 0 6 *